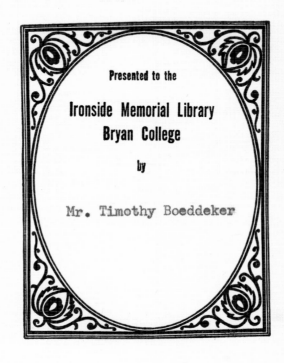

THE OTTOMAN
IMPACT
ON EUROPE

THE OTTOMAN
IMPACT
ON EUROPE

PAUL COLES

with 109 illustrations, 16 in color

HARCOURT, BRACE & WORLD, INC.

First American Edition 1968

Library of Congress Catalog Card Number: 68–20630

PRINTED IN GREAT BRITAIN BY JARROLD AND SONS LTD NORWICH

CONTENTS

'Modern history', wrote Lord Acton, 'begins under stress of the Ottoman conquest.' This book elaborates and explores Lord Acton's judgment.

Chronologically it runs from the mid-fourteenth century, when the Ottomans broke into Europe and the danger which they represented was abruptly revealed to the consciousness of Europeans, to the late seventeenth, when the failure of the second siege of Vienna (1683) and the Treaty of Karlowitz (1699) marked the beginnings of the long, slow retreat of the Turks from their European conquests. Within these limits the years from the 1520s to the 1580s receive special attention as the period when the Turkish threat was at its gravest and most intense.

Ottoman inroads forked into two large adjacent theatres of action: eastern – Danubian, Balkan and Pontic – Europe; and the Mediterranean basin. Developments in these regions dominate the narrative. This is, therefore, essentially an essay in frontier history; but, since the struggle often reached or reverberated beyond the zones of direct conflict, a wider frame of reference is frequently invoked.

The narrative surface is inevitably much concerned with war. However, I have tried throughout to interpret this material as a register of contrasting societies in process of collision, interpenetration and change.

Miss Joan Barrass, Information Officer of the University of Bradford, typed several drafts of the manuscript and checked innumerable references with unfailing speed and precision. Her criticisms also led to the removal of many faults of construction and infelicities of style.

I am also greatly indebted to Mr Ronald Davidson-Houston of Thames and Hudson for the assembly and selection of the illustrations. Mr Stanley Baron has been a patient and helpful editor.

7

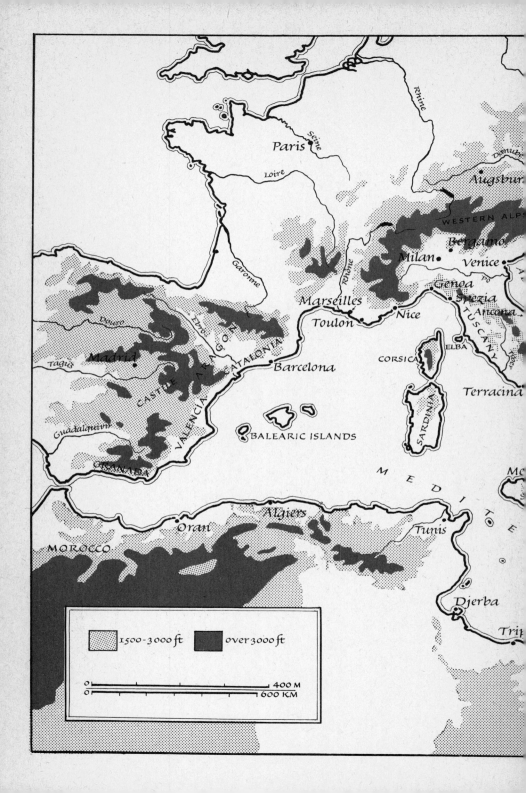

Paris

Seine

Loire

Rhine

Danube

Augsbur.

WESTERN ALPS

Garonne

Bergamo

Milan

Venice

Rhône

Genoa

Spezia

Ancona

Duero

Marseilles

Nice

TUSCANY

Toulon

Ebro

CASTILE

ARAGON

CATALONIA

Tagus

Madrid

CORSICA

ELBA

Barcelona

Guadalquivir

VALENCIA

SARDINIA

Terracina

GRANADA

BALEARIC ISLANDS

M E D I T E

Mo

Algiers

Oran

Tunis

MOROCCO

Djerba

Trip

1500-3000 ft   over 3000 ft

0   400 M
0   600 KM

1 The severity and majesty of the Ottoman ruling class is illustrated in this sixteenth-century European portrait, which probably represents Sultan Suleiman the Magnificent

I THE EMERGENCE OF OTTOMAN POWER

The dominant theme of the half millennium which began about the year AD 1000 was the outpouring of Turkish and Mongolian peoples from the Eurasian steppe. Infiltration or conquest by these barbarian nomads affected almost the entire civilized world. Only poor and peripheral areas, scarcely worth the exertions of conquest, such as Japan or the medieval European west, escaped political dominion by steppe warriors. In geographical scope only the conquests of the bronze-working charioteers of the eighteenth to fifteenth centuries BC can compare with this ethnic inundation.

But the long-established and deep-rooted Moslem civilization of the Middle East proved capable of absorbing and incorporating these intruders. Islamic societies, which suffered terribly from nomad infiltration and conquest, nevertheless profited from the upheaval of traditional relationships which the steppe invasions brought in their wake. To be sure, a far-reaching internal transformation of Islamic society was necessary before a more or less satisfactory *modus vivendi* could be established between the new Turkish rulers and the older civilized peoples of the Middle East. Yet once this had been accomplished, the military prowess of the converted steppe invaders, together with the new missionary energy generated by the Sufi movement (see p. 63) led to a remarkable expansion which carried Islam far beyond its classical frontiers; on the one hand into India, China and the East Indies and, on the other, into Asia Minor and eastern Europe. One aspect of this process was the impact upon Europe of a tidal wave of Turkish conquest.

By AD 1000 the so-called steppe gradient had been in continuous operation for thirteen or fourteen centuries, compelling one central Asian tribe after another to seek better pastures in more favourable western environments. The effect was to establish an ethnic and linguistic drift across Asia, as first Indo-Europeans, then Turks, then Mongols and finally Turks again, migrated westwards. Yet, while languages changed, in all this time the essential economic, political and military pattern of horse nomadry altered very little.

Nevertheless, knowledge of civilized ways had now penetrated with a new intensity among the tribesmen of the steppe. Closer relations with urban and agricultural populations always held great attractions for nomadic groups, for whom cereals, textiles and metals offered a welcome supplement to the sparse resources provided by pastoralism and hunting. As more frequent commercial contacts and experience of mercenary service in civilized armies gave the barbarian tribes an enhanced awareness of the wealth and wonders of the southern civilizations, the gravitational pull of China, the Middle East and Byzantium upon the formidable horsemen of the steppe inevitably increased.

The infiltration of nomad groups into the settled regions was easiest in the Middle East, where agricultural land shaded off by almost imperceptible degrees into parched grassland. There the nomads could continue their accustomed mode of life on the margin of settled society and graze the stubble after harvesting, while simultaneously enjoying the luxuries obtained through trade or tributary relationships with farming or urban populations. Thus the line between steppe and sown land became increasingly blurred; and in the course of time Turkish-speaking groups extensively penetrated Iranian populations. These Turks accepted the Moslem faith and adopted Islamic customs and manners; but they never entirely submerged themselves in the Moslem world. A sense of superiority, based upon pride in their military techniques and prowess, kept them from full assimilation; and they retained their language, together with much of the warlike ethos of the steppe.

2 A nomad encampment. Its origins as a primitive nomadic warband bequeathed to the Ottoman state an appetite for plunder which proved difficult to adapt to the growth of imperial institutions and responsibilities

13

Two adventitious factors facilitated Turkish incorporation into the Moslem world as a distinct, yet scarcely alien people, and contributed decisively to Turkish military and political success in the Middle East. One was the fact that when the Turks first emerged as a formidable element within the body politic of Islam, Shi'a rulers were almost everywhere dominant (see pp. 63 ff.). In consequence, when Turkish rulers embraced Islam, they tended to choose its Sunnite form, thereby asserting their independence from the civilized authorities closest to them. But Sunnite doctrine had been the orthodoxy of the great days of the early caliphate and was still the faith of the majority of Moslems. Hence, in submitting to Turkish rule, many Moslems felt that they were repudiating heresy and reviving the glories of the past.

The second factor was the Moslem concept of Holy War (*Jihad*) waged by *ghazis*, special champions of the Faith, whose courage in battle constituted a sort of sanctity. Warfare across the frontiers of Islam therefore offered rude Turks an honourable role which was exactly suited to their warlike traditions. Although prospects of plunder and self-aggrandizement doubtless provided a stronger motivation for most Turks than piety and the service of Allah, the ideal of the Holy War made it comparatively easy to find an honorific place for Turkish warriors within Islam and enabled civilized Moslems to deflect Turkish military enterprise against their Hindu and Christian neighbours.

The result of these geographical, religious and cultural circumstances was therefore to permit the massive incorporation of Turkish societies into Islam. Turks provided a majority of Moslem rulers and soldiers from the eleventh century onwards, and constituted the cutting edge of Islamic expansion into both Hindustan and Christendom.

The assumption by Turks of political dominion over the Islamic world occupied the eleventh to thirteenth centuries. Interrupted by the period of Mongol conquest initiated by Ghengis Khan (1206–27), Turkish domination was revived and resumed during the fourteenth and fifteenth centuries. The arrival in the Middle East of waves of Turkish invaders from the steppe inflicted severe economic damage and political disorder upon the Moslem core area; yet it stimulated rather than hindered the expansion of Islam. Incessant warfare in the Moslem heartlands produced a continuous stream of seasoned soldiers eager to do battle for plunder and the true faith against Christendom. Political disorder at the centre of Islam thus operated as a great winnowing fan, sucking warriors from the steppe into the Moslem heartland and impelling the survivors outwards across the frontiers. Given this basic mechanism of social forces, prodigious opportunities awaited any Moslem dynasty capable of stabilizing the political situation in the Middle East, submitting the furious energies of the Moslem world to the will of a single authority and constructing a war machine of unparalleled power for the prosecution of the *Jihad* against the Christian west. Such absolute and undivided authority was never, in fact, established; but its partial achievement by the Ottoman sultans provides both a measure of their greatness and an explanation of their success.

One consequence of the extreme violence and instability which characterized the Moslem world of the Middle East before the advent of the Ottomans was the devastation of the traditional heartlands of Islam. Iraq and Syria suffered severely, while the previously secondary, but now less disturbed areas, in particular Anatolia, attained much greater importance. This shift of the centre of economic gravity to an area immediately adjacent to Byzantium, having easy access to western Christendom, favoured the emergence in this region of a major Moslem power capable of organizing and launching a sustained and ferocious onslaught across the western frontiers of Islam.

Anatolia (Asia Minor), once a rich Roman province, fell into political decline as the Roman empire itself decayed, being ravaged by pestilence and malaria and by Persian and Arab invaders in the seventh and eighth centuries. Its prosperity was restored by the reviving Byzantine empire in the ninth century, from which time it was developed, under close imperial supervision, as the economic platform of Byzantine power and prosperity. Anatolian fruit, grain, olives and meat sustained the whole empire and Anatolian peasants provided the backbone of Byzantine armies. During the tenth century the frontiers of this region came under acute pressure from tribes moving out of the desiccating plains of Turkestan. The crushing defeat of Byzantine forces at the hands of these interlopers at the battle of Manzikert (1071) opened a new period which saw a steady contraction of Byzantine territory under the encroachments of Turkish border barons who, as the instruments of this pressure, were designated *ghazis* by the Seljuk sultans who struggled with some initial success to knit the turbulent Turkish invaders into a confederation under their own suzerainty. During the thirteenth century disaster impartially overtook both Seljuk sultans and Byzantine emperors. Byzantium never recovered from the events of 1204, when in response to Venetian promptings the participants in the Fourth Crusade seized and sacked the capital. Thereafter the Greek and Balkan provinces fell away; and these catastrophes were compounded by the ravages of the Black Death which decimated the population of the empire during the late 1340s.

At the same time, the efforts of the Seljuk sultans to impose discipline on the Turkish tribes were nullified by the depredations of the Mongols, who launched savage if transient raids and expeditions into Asia Minor, which weakened and eventually extinguished Seljuk power. This freed the *ghazi* border chieftains from the last restraints of central authority. Reinforced by a perpetual stream of refugees from Mongol rule, they renewed pressure on the Byzantine frontiers and prepared – in cases where this was geographically possible – to launch themselves into eastern Europe.

Among the numerous *ghazi* emirates which sprang up from the ruins of older and larger Anatolian political systems in the second half of the thirteenth century was that founded by Ertughrul (d. 1281) in the hinterland behind the town of Brusa, which overlooked the Sea of Marmora. This was the origin of the Ottoman state. The minuscule principality possessed two advantages. In the first place, it was geographically remote both from the major zone of Mongol invasion and from the already powerful Turkish emirates of south and south-western Anatolia. Secondly, it was the only Turkish outpost still facing unconquered Byzantine territory (elsewhere the Turks had already reached the coast). It thus exercised a

3, 4 Sultans Orkhan (left) and Murad I (right). These sixteenth-century European portraits transform the fourteenth-century *ghazi* leaders into the remote and opulent rulers of contemporary western imagination

magnetic attraction upon a stream of adventurers and refugees – Turkish mercenaries drawn by opportunities for booty, dervishes in search of disciples, land-hungry cultivators fleeing before the Mongols. As other *ghazi* leaders quarrelled among themselves over the partition of occupied Byzantine territory, Ottoman rulers were still able to offer the prospect of land or plunder to all who accepted their command. This social magnetism and expansive impetus enabled the Ottomans both to expand their control over Asia Minor and to erupt into the Balkans.

The creation of an Ottoman state of impressive proportions posed the problems of sustaining aggressive impulses while transforming a turbulent *ghazi* empire into a more settled and rational community. This was the achievement of the Sultans Orkhan (1326–62) and Murad I (1362–89). The capture of large towns (Brusa in 1326; Nicaea in 1329; Nicomedia in 1337; and, in Europe, Adrianople in 1354) anchored the empire to urban points of order. Ottoman encouragement of the influence of representatives of orthodox Sunnite Islam

5 The growth of an elaborate chancery accompanied the consolidation of the Ottoman Empire. The *tughra*, or personal emblem, of Suleiman the Magnificent heads the text of this edict, or *firman*, 1562

against that of the heterodox and unreliable dervish elements had two important results: it ensured a relative degree of religious toleration for Christian subjects and thus reduced objections to Ottoman rule among Orthodox Christian peasant populations in Asia Minor and the Balkans; and it allowed the establishment of mosque schools, factories of the *ulema*, the experts in Moslem theology and law whose training and disciplinarian instincts provided the nucleus of a rudimentary civil service.

Most important of all were reforms in the military system. The earliest instrument of Ottoman power and expansion was the 'horde', the body of volunteer nomad light cavalry which was the natural military formation of the fighting peoples of the steppe. This was gradually replaced by the practice of allotting fiefs (*timars*) to Turkish cavalrymen, among whom 'feudal' gradations of property and titles were now introduced. This reform simultaneously bound the cavalryman irreversibly to the sultan and whetted his appetite for further conquest. The mounted force thus created was balanced and supplemented by the creation of the janissary corps of paid household infantry, slaves in status, recruited or pressed into service from Christian or ex-Christian subject populations. From a very early period a striking feature of Islamic society had been the widespread use of slave soldiery to support the personal power of the ruler. A monarch whose control over the state might be challenged by unruly citizens or a free warrior aristocracy found it tempting to expand and arm his household until his personal slaves became a standing army. Turks had themselves filled the role of slave soldiers under the Abbasid Caliph Mutasim (833–42), who initiated the system, and under many of his subsequent Middle Eastern imitators. Themselves now graduated to the position of overlords, they devolved the obligations and the opportunities of such service upon their newly conquered subjects. The elaboration of this system was not complete until the mid-fifteenth century, by which time the slave family of the sultan had become a major source of administrators as well as soldiers.

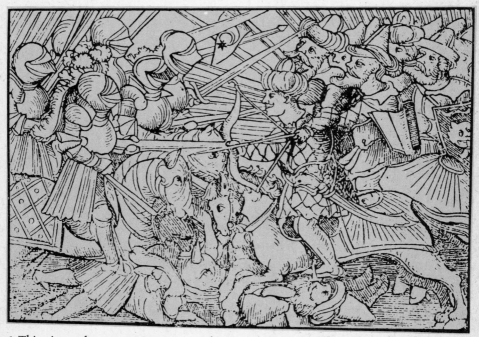

6 This sixteenth-century German woodcut contrasts the lightly armoured but mobile Turkish horsemen with the ponderous Christian cavalry. (See the quotation from Fynes Moryson on pp. 99–100)

Efficient in isolation, the *timar* and janissary systems were even more potent in combination; for they created a permanent tension between the major components of the Ottoman armed forces – 'free' cavalrymen against slave infantry – which could be exploited by rulers to their personal advantage. The social necessity of some authority capable of maintaining balance and discipline between these elements was one powerful source of the absolute character of the Ottoman sultans' rule.

In transition from nomadic horde to Ottoman empire, the reign of Orkhan seems to have been crucial; and the most apt symbol of the whole process was the inscription referring to himself which he placed in the new mosque in conquered Brusa. This stressed the continuing *ghazi* character of the new state and also marked the first formal assumption by an Ottoman emir of the 'imperial' title of Sultan: 'Sultan, son of the Sultan of the Ghazis, Ghazi, son of Ghazis, Margrave of the horizons, hero of the world.'

It was Orkhan, too, who led his people towards their first conquest in Europe. Transported from Asia in 1345 as mercenaries in Byzantine pay, the Ottomans quickly broke free from imperial control. By the 1350s they were moving into Europe as independent invaders and settlers, occupying Gallipoli and Adrianople, colonizing the European coast of the Sea of Marmora and pressing into Thrace and the Morea. In 1363 they were recognized in their possessions by the Byzantine emperor. From these vantage points the Ottomans fanned out into the vacuum left in south-eastern Europe by the decline of Byzantine authority. By the end of the decade they had established themselves in Bulgaria and reached the Danube and the Rhodope mountains. This brought them into confrontation with their first highly organized European opposition, the Serbian empire.

The central episodes in the long history of Ottoman success in the Balkans between the fourteenth and the seventeenth centuries were the destruction of two considerable Christian states, Serbia in the late fourteenth century and Hungary in the early sixteenth. Given the local ebb and flow of conflict and the delays caused by the fact that on numerous occasions Turkish interests and energies were distracted elsewhere, interstitial conquests inevitably followed these spectacular victories. The collapse of Serbia sealed the fate of Byzantium and provided a dress rehearsal for the overthrow of Hungary.

Yet in the mid-fourteenth century the Turks were only beginning to encroach into eastern Europe and were still far from controlling the whole of Asia Minor. At this point the very large, aggressive and apparently powerful Serbian empire seemed far likelier than that of the Ottomans to capture Constantinople and enter upon the Byzantine inheritance. It also seemed likely to provide an effective European bulwark against further Turkish advance.

The ancient kingdom of Serbia had been a small client state of Byzantium, sandwiched between the latter (whose territory included modern Macedonia), Hungary (which then included modern Bosnia, Croatia and the north bank of the Danube) and Bulgaria (which then included Niš and adjacent lands to the west). The thirteenth-century decline of Byzantium allowed the reconstitution of Serbia around a new capital, Uskub (the modern Skopje). From

7 Sultan Murad I was assassinated in obscure circumstances immediately after he had destroyed the remnants of Serbian resistance at the first battle of Kossovo (1389). His mausoleum (below) was erected on the scene of his triumph

21

this centre Serbia expanded rapidly under the energetic rule of Stephan Dušan (1331–55) who assumed the title 'Tsar of the Serbs and the Greeks', annexed all Macedonia, Thrace, Epirus and Thessaly, reduced Bulgaria to dependency and pushed his dominions to the Mediterranean coast opposite Corfu and to the Aegean at Salonika. Stephan Dušan established a brilliant pseudo-Byzantine political and religious system. The Serbian church was reorganized and revived to support the new regime. Greek was adopted as the administrative language and Byzantine-trained bureaucrats were recruited into the civil service. The edifice was crowned by the promulgation of a celebrated code of laws, the *Dušanov Zakonik*, in 1349.

Yet this imposing structure proved to be a phantom empire. The extreme fragility – soon to be cruelly exposed by mounting Ottoman pressure – was characteristic of the fissiparous society which emerged in the vacuum caused by the relaxation of Byzantine rule. The adoption of a Byzantine cultural style masked, without eliminating, the centrifugal social tendencies represented by unruly, unreliable and self-interested feudal magnates. Many of the latter defected to the Ottoman sultan during the crisis of 1389. Even the *Dušanov Zakonik* proves on close inspection to have been feudal in its basic assumptions, Byzantine merely in the forms of its expression. Urban centres – Ohrid, Salonika, Kavala – stubbornly resisted incorporation into a centralized territorial state. Internal social conflicts between nobility and peasants were sharpened as a result of the incidence of the Black Death after 1347, when a drastic reduction of the labour force increased the severity of aristocratic demands and exactions.

The impressive bulk of the Serbian empire also distracted attention from its strategic weakness. The state rested upon dominion over two intersecting routes of trade and communication: the east to west artery from Ragusa (Dubrovnik) through Novibazar, Niš, Sofia, Philippopolis and Adrianople (Edirne) to Constantinople; and the north to south (Morava-Vardar) corridor, which linked the confluence of the Danube and Sava at Belgrade with the Aegean at Salonika. The essential axis of empire, the cross-roads area of these routes, was easily accessible to invaders from north, west and south;

8, 9 A contemporary MS of the codex of Stephan Dušan (left). The crown, sceptre and vestments in the portrait of the 'Tsar' (right) illustrate his deliberate and ruinously expensive imitation of the forms and conventions of Byzantine imperialism

and once this zone was lost the whole dependent structure could simply be commandeered, with no inaccessible refuge areas available capable of sustaining resistance or counter-attack, and no profound local loyalties on which Serbian rulers might, in defeat, rely.

In this social and geographical situation, the sole effective solution available to the Serbian monarchy for its problems was that which later confronted Hungary in the early sixteenth century: the creation of an effective mercenary army. But Serbian resources were dissipated on expensive Byzantine imitations: court ceremonial, ecclesiastical architecture and an interminable bureaucracy. Such luxuries remained tolerable while the plunder of the borderlands was available for the sustenance of military professionals; but the conquests of Stephan Dušan reached the limits of expansion – and consequently of plunder – when they brought the Serbian empire into contact and eventual violent collision with an Ottoman system which had already interposed itself between Serbia and the next logical victim, Byzantium. Riven by separatism and faction after the death of Stephan Dušan in 1355, Serbia was overwhelmed by the Turks. The Serbians were defeated on the Maritza River in 1371 with the loss of much of Bulgaria and most of Macedonia. Niš fell to the Ottomans in 1387. Finally, a Serbian alliance was destroyed at the first battle of Kossovo in 1389. The Turks now began to consolidate their Balkan conquests by the detailed and systematic occupation of Greece and Bulgaria. And in 1396 they turned back to concentrate upon important unfinished business in Asia Minor: the siege of Constantinople and the elimination of the Byzantine empire.

The Burgundian and allied contingents of the Crusade of Nicopolis (1396) forced the sultan to abandon the first siege of Constantinople, though the crusaders themselves were defeated by Ottoman forces. A second siege in 1402 was raised when the Mongol conqueror, Timur (Tamerlane), briefly invaded Asia Minor. The chaos which Timur left in his wake confronted the Ottomans with a serious and prolonged problem of re-establishing their dominion in that region. These distractions permitted a revival of resistance to Ottoman advance in eastern Europe, inspired by the tribal chieftain Scanderbeg in Albania and by John Hunyadi of Transylvania, regent of Hungary. Only after the defeat of Hunyadi at the second battle

10 Scanderbeg ('Alexander Beg', d. 1467), an Albanian nobleman, spent his youth at the Ottoman court. He deserted the Ottoman cause for that of Christianity, and with papal assistance inspired prolonged Albanian resistance to Turkish invasion

◀ 11 The Transylvanian war-lord, John
Hunyadi, regent of Hungary (d. 1458,
opposite), assembled a group of client
states round the Hungarian kingdom.
Defeated several times in battle, he
nevertheless succeeded in frustrating an
attempt by the Sultan Mohammed the
Conqueror to capture Belgrade in 1456

12 Fifteenth-century Turkish expansion at
the expense of Christian powers was
frequently interrupted by the inroads of
Mongol invaders into Ottoman Asia
Minor. This sixteenth-century Persian
painting shows the Ottoman Sultan
Bayazid I humbling himself before the
Mongol emperor Timur

of Kossovo in 1448 were the Turks again free to besiege the Byzantine capital. The city was invested in 1451 and fell in 1453.

The downfall of Byzantium sent a stream of refugees and tremors of fear, shock and despair throughout Christendom. The permanence of Ottoman conquests in Europe was now guaranteed by the elimination of the only strategic base which Christendom could use against the Turks. Equally, the predominance of the Ottoman empire over the Mamaluke kingdom in Egypt and Syria was now assured, though Cairo was not formally subjected to Constantinople until 1516–17, when Sultan Selim the Grim finally broke Mamaluke resistance in battle. But from the Ottoman standpoint the capture of Constantinople was much more than a major military triumph. The city was a great metropolis, the centre of an extensive network of trade, communication and administration, which had decayed in recent centuries, but could now be reanimated to the advantage of the Turks. Situated at the principal point of intersection between Europe and Asia, it was the natural capital for an empire whose provinces reached into both continents. Despite the acquisition of numerous urban centres during the conquests of the fourteenth and early fifteenth centuries and the stabilizing administrative reforms of Orkhan and Murad I, the Ottomans could still be described, before 1453, as essentially an oriental 'horde' operating within a fairly fluid zone of depredation and conquest. With the entry into Constantinople, the Ottoman state was transformed into one of the great historic imperialisms, a work of art as well as a force of nature. This process of consolidation was most evident in the expansion and elaboration of the sultan's slave household which followed during the second half of the fifteenth century. This was the era in which the child tribute of the Balkans was organized on a grand scale to satisfy the empire's appetite for soldiers and administrators.

Not only did the new task of sustaining a great capital enormously increase the demand for slaves as household troops, servants, concubines and functionaries; the capture of Constantinople, by conferring dominion over the narrow entrance to the Black Sea, also provided the Ottomans with the key to a huge new reservoir of food supplies and slave manpower. During the early fifteenth century

26

13 *Devshirme*, the Turkish practice of taking children as slaves in lieu of taxes from poor and remote Balkan provinces, began in the early fifteenth century. Many of the ablest Ottoman generals and administrators were the products of this system, which was discontinued in 1638 ▶

Greek and Genoese merchant colonies on the coasts of the Black Sea plied a rich trade with Europe in grain, horses, lead, fish and occasionally south Russian slaves. Once established in Constantinople, the Ottomans throttled this commerce, then diverted the fish, grain and timber of Pontic Europe to sustain Constantinople and build a formidable navy. In 1475 Turkish warships captured Caffa,

14 Parmigianino's portrait of a Turkish slave girl illustrates the material compensations which frequently accompanied servile status in Ottoman society

15 This illustration to a French work of 1455 shows the close investment of Constantinople by Ottoman land and sea forces on the eve of the final assault in 1453 ▶

the principal Genoese outpost, and other key ports on the Black Sea. The Crimean Tartars of the hinterland to the north were obliged to adapt themselves to the formidable new occupants of the coastal towns. From the 1480s Tartar slave raids into Poland and the Ukraine assumed massive proportions, the victims of these expeditions being shipped south in droves from the Black Sea ports to Constantinople, there to serve the pleasure, pride and imperial purposes of the conquerors.

Byzantium had been a second Rome in terms not only of political, but also of ecclesiastical organization; and the inability of the Greek Orthodox Church to come to terms with the Papacy was an important cause of the failure of the great powers of the Christian West to move to the relief of the expiring empire during the siege of 1451–3. With the capture of the city, the destiny of Greek Orthodox Christianity passed into Ottoman proprietorship. The

response of Mohammed II the Conqueror to this situation was a measure of how far and how rapidly the Ottoman rulers had progressed from their *ghazi* origins.

We have seen how, in attempting to convert a freebooters' frontier principality into a great Moslem empire, the earlier Ottoman sultans called in the help of the *ulema*. This had two curious effects. On the one hand, by enhancing the place of the Sacred Law in Ottoman life, the *ulema* widened the breach between Moslems and Christians – a breach which had been minimal in the first phase of Ottoman expansion when the heterodoxies of the Sufi movement often overlapped with Christian doctrine. Secondly, however, the Sacred Law itself inculcated toleration for the 'Peoples of the Book' and forbade forcible interference with the Christian or Jewish religions, thus restraining *ghazi* impulses of headlong attack upon any and all infidels. Hence, as the rude frontiersmen of early Ottoman history gave ground before the sultan's slave household and the orthodox *ulema* of Sunnite Islam, conversion of Christian subjects was reduced, save for individual instances, to the limited channel of the slave household itself. Only in remote and mountainous regions like Bosnia, where the prevalence of the Manichean sect of Bogomilism probably facilitated the reception of Islam, or in Crete or Albania, where incessant local warfare fostered a spirit resembling that of the old *ghazis*, did significant conversion from Christianity to Islam occur after the fourteenth century.

These circumstances presented an obvious danger that the Ottoman empire would prove incapable of incorporating the mass of Orthodox Christian subjects acquired by conquest in the Balkans. The capture of Constantinople offered a convenient solution to this problem. The city was the seat of the Greek Orthodox patriarch. Mohammed the Conqueror established the popular and bitterly anti-Catholic monk, Gennadios, in this office, confirming and extending the prerogatives and immunities which the Orthodox Church had enjoyed under the Byzantine empire. The patriarch was entrusted with wide judicial powers, especially in the field of family law, over all Christian subjects of the sultan. In effect, Mohammed was regularizing a double regime. The Christian clergy

16 The Bogomils, a sect named after its founder, the priest Bogomil – a Slavonic translation of the Greek Theophilus – held that the material world was the creation of the devil, and regarded with equal detestation the Roman and Greek Orthodox versions of Christianity. They were largely swallowed up into the Moslem world, leaving only scatterings of curious funeral monuments, such as that illustrated, in Bosnia and Herzegovina

became a mirror image of the *ulema*, exercising an authority over Christians comparable to that which the legal and theological experts of Islam wielded over Moslems. Conversely, the sultan imitated Christian practice by organizing a regular hierarchy among the *ulema* and subjecting them to a more rigorous government control than any previous Moslem ruler had done. To this extent the stability of the Ottoman state was improved and the sultan's personal power increased.

31

II STRUCTURE OF THE OTTOMAN EMPIRE

Although this book is concerned with the effects of the great age of Ottoman conquest upon Europe rather than with the domestic history of the Ottoman empire, in fact the two themes are inseparable. The structure and evolution of Ottoman social institutions helped to determine the particular form and extent of Ottoman influence.

At the end of our period, the close of the seventeenth century, the expansive thrust and power so characteristic of the Ottoman system at its point of maximum success was quite exhausted. Turkish society was either fossilized or, in some sectors, undergoing a painful process of acculturation which brought it into approximate conformity with the bureaucratic monarchies then prevailing in the West. But during the fifteenth and sixteenth centuries this empire, in which deliberate administrative contrivance blended so curiously with ungovernable social impulses, differed in almost every essential respect from the European societies upon which it impinged. Any analysis of the structure of the Ottoman empire in this period must concentrate upon these differences.

The very use of the term 'structure' may seem to imply exclusive concern with what was permanent, or at least enduring, rather than with institutions or arrangements which were in process of rapid evolution. This is not necessarily so. In the history of the Ottoman empire until the late seventeenth century change is the dominant and inescapable motif; the pattern of events is shot through with movement, action, dramatic enterprise, triumph and disaster. In these conditions the character of social groups and institutions changed rapidly, as did the complex of relationships between them. When we speak, therefore, of examining the structure of the empire, we should be clear that it is only profitable to do so by delineating

33

17 Scene of investiture on the Persian frontier, late sixteenth century. Sultan Murad III (ruled 1574–95) stands beneath the canopy. This miniature, the work of a Turkish artist strongly influenced by Persian traditions, illustrates the extent to which the primitive freebooting instincts of the early Ottoman state evolved into a highly formalized imperialism

the composition and interplay of a field of social forces rather than by describing external forms and official procedures. History is not made by committees, but rather by the social pressures and pulsations which manufacture and regulate them. These are the true structural factors.

Ottoman society revolved around and was shaped by the central institution of the sultanate. Historically the institution of monarchy has a three-fold root: in the monarch's role as leader in battle, as law-giver and as ecclesiastical official. Ottoman sultans functioned in all these capacities.

Uninterrupted conquest was the law of life of Turkish society; the sultans emerged into the light of recorded history as leaders of a *ghazi* horde. Even when the empire had acquired a metropolis and was governed through a formal and elaborate administrative system, it remained almost continuously at war, a vast encampment rather than a state in the European sense. Until the advent of a succession of luxurious and *fainéant* rulers in the later sixteenth century, sultans were active field commanders, usually quitting Constantinople with the army each spring and campaigning throughout the summer. It is instructive to compare the peregrinations of a great sixteenth-century sultan, Suleiman the Magnificent, with those of a prominent contemporary European ruler, the Emperor Charles V. Charles never shrank from the obligations of generalship; but the essential pattern of his journeyings is that of a monarch intent on strengthening or repairing the web of government which spanned and connected his scattered dominions. He plodded conscientiously from one regional capital to another, surrounded by bureaucrats, showing himself to his subjects, holding court, receiving couriers, pondering petitions and conducting correspondence. Suleiman, in contrast, spent only the winter months in administrative activities, seldom stirring at this time of year from Constantinople to visit the provincial capitals. Yet each summer found him far from the metropolis, with the army on the frontiers of his empire; fortresses and battlegrounds rather than townships and administrative centres marked the stages of his progress.

In the scroll: SVLTAN SOLIMAN Imperador de Turchi Entro al gouerno L'anno 1519 et mori L'anno 1566

18, 19 Rival champions of European and Ottoman imperialism: the Holy Roman Emperor Charles V (left) and the Ottoman Sultan Suleiman I the Magnificent

As *ghazi* chieftains, the earliest Ottomans were law-givers only in the sense that they took the necessary peremptory decisions, resolving disputes or dividing booty amongst their followers, dispensing the rough justice essential to maintain the cohesion and momentum of a predatory horde. But the policy, adopted by the sultans of the fourteenth and fifteenth centuries, of close association with the *ulema*, the theologians and jurists expert in the interpretation of the *Shari'a* or Sacred Law of Islam and the principal representatives of Sunnite orthodoxy, transformed the situation. In

35

Islamic civilization no distinction was drawn between the law-giving and the priestly-ecclesiastical functions. Mohammed had ruled Medina and Mecca using local customary law when he thought it good, but relying on his own judgment when that seemed to him better. What he bequeathed to succeeding generations of Moslems was not so much a legal code as a series of judgments arranged in the accidental sequence of their delivery. These covered subjects as diverse as prayer, ritual ablution, the distribution of alms, fasting, pilgrimage, business transactions, inheritance, marriage, divorce, the use of intoxicants, the holy war, hunting, horse-racing, vows of obedience and slavery. The result was a complicated but unsystem-atized battery of regulations. These regulations were something more than laws in the conventional and constricted western sense; they also had the force of binding religious edicts. A modern scholar, D. B. Macdonald, summarizes the situation as follows:

> Muslim law, in the most absolute sense, fits the old definition, and is the science of all things, human and divine . . . it takes all duty for its portion and defines all action in terms of duty. Nothing can escape the narrow meshes of its net. One of the greatest legists of Islam never ate a water melon because he could not find that the usage of the Prophet had laid down and sanctioned a canonical method of doing so.

By patronizing the *ulema* the Ottoman sultans installed themselves at the head of a legal and theological hierarchy which wielded immense powers over every field of human conduct. This added religious prestige and authority to their position, which they were careful to extend and exploit whenever possible. In 1538 Suleiman added the title of Caliph – literally 'successor' (to the Prophet) – to the long catalogue of his dignities. In 1683 even Mohammed IV, who was less than preoccupied by affairs of state, interrupted his obsessional routine of hunting in order to travel into Hungary to perform the important ecclesiastical function of investing the Grand Vizier Kara Mustapha with the robe of gold and the standard of Mohammed, thus constituting him official leader of Islam in the Holy War against Christianity.

20 Claims to descent from or legitimate succession to the Prophet were an important source of political authority in the Islamic world. This genealogy of Mohammed (veiled) was commissioned by his namesake, the Ottoman Sultan Mohammed III ▶

قصي
عبد مناف
عبد الشمس
اميه
حرب
ابو سفيان
معاويه
يزيد
عبد الملك
عفان
عباس
حضرت عباس
حضرت ابی طالب
حضرت عبد الله
حضرت حمزه
کعب
سعد
عامر
خطاب
نفيل
عبد العزى
رباح
عبد الله
مرزبان
مادان
خرخيره
قباد
بلاش
پرويز
هرمزد
يزدجرد

21 A Turkish armourer
wearing the uniform
of his gild

To a certain extent the theocratic system which they operated imprisoned as much as it empowered the Ottoman sultans, for no ruler could alter or violate the *Shari'a*. Imperial edicts were therefore primarily interpretative in character, adapting the received law to new needs and changed circumstances. But within these limits much could be achieved. Suleiman the Magnificent was the most active, conscientious and influential administrator of all the sultans, issuing a mass of detailed regulations (*firmans*) concerning landholding, the inheritance of property, the duties of public officials and the conditions of military service. To his subjects he was known as *Kanuni*, 'the law-maker'. And even though the sultans admitted the primacy of the *Shari'a* and the obligations of the ruler in relation to it, Ottoman society harboured few of the vested interests and points of resistance to the free exercise of monarchical power which existed so abundantly in Europe. The general weakness and fragility of family ties in the principle of absolute equality between all true believers and the uninheritable nature of fiefs distributed under the *timar* system all worked against the evolution of a rooted territorial aristocracy with particularist interests and social pretensions which were opposed to the centralizing policy of the government. The urban populations and fighting forces of the empire were conveniently organized in a system of gilds and confraternities; such were the *akhis*, associations of merchants and artisans, and the *levend*, confraternities of seamen and corsairs. The janissaries of Constantinople, the Mamaluke infantry of Egypt, even the *ulema*, who supplied many judges and administrators, were similarly organized. Each of these gilds was a Moslem 'mystery' as well as a secular association, appointing its own spiritual advisers; and, since the sultan headed and directed the religious hierarchy, they formed collectively a tissue of powerful and influential brotherhoods which were, in general, responsive and obedient to the requirements of the head of the state.

Strong Moslem traditions also sanctified unquestioning submission to the sultan: 'the apostle of God said: after me will come rulers; render them your obedience.' Even if a monarch was recognizably tyrannical and unjust, his overthrow was the business of Allah, not that of the subject:

if they are righteous and rule you well, they shall have their reward; but if they do evil and rule you ill, then punishment will fall upon them and you will be quit of it.

In both theory and practice, therefore, the will of the Ottoman sultans of the fifteenth and sixteenth centuries was absolute and compelling beyond the wildest hopes and imagination of contemporary European rulers. Some remarks of Suleiman to the Austrian ambassador in 1534 concerning the disputed kingdom of Hungary well illustrate his consciousness of possessing a plenitude of power:

This realm belongs to me and I have set therein my servant . . . I have given him this kingdom, I can take it back from him, if I wish, for mine is the right to dispose of it and of all its inhabitants, who are my subjects.

39

22, 23 Sultan Mohammed II 'the Conqueror' of Constantinople; and Selim I 'the Grim', who added Syria and Egypt to the Ottoman empire

This unique concentration of authority was exercised through a system of government whose architect was Sultan Mohammed II, the Conqueror, whose *Kanoun Namé*, or fundamental law, promulgated after the capture of Constantinople, codified the experiments and initiatives of his predecessors. From this document derived the sanction which permitted the murder of the sultan's relatives in order to guarantee a smooth succession. The throne was universally agreed to be hereditary in the Ottoman ruling house; but the polygamous marriage customs of Islam and the absence from Moslem law of any principle of inheritance by the eldest male heir presented the recurrent problem of contending claims to the succession being simultaneously advanced by several sons of the sultan. During the last years of the reign of Suleiman this represented such a danger to the stability of the state that the sultan was obliged to execute two of his sons, Mustapha in 1553 and Bayazid in 1561, in order to ensure the succession for the sole survivor, Selim. Such disturbances before the death of a sultan were unavoidable; but at least the further possibility of usurpation could be, and was, ruled

24 Members of the gild of sweepers prepare the Hippodrome at Constantinople
under the stern eye of Sultan Murad III. In contrast to slaves and renegades of
Christian origin, who virtually monopolized the high offices of state, Moslem-born
subjects of the Ottoman empire seldom advanced beyond their original station in life

25 *Kazi-Asker*. This high official, one of the few who were invariably Moslem by birth, directed and controlled the Ottoman legal system

out by sanctioning the practice whereby a new sultan, on ascending the throne, executed all his brothers and their male children. This custom prevailed until the seventeenth century, when, probably under the influence of European example, the throne usually passed into the possession of the sultan's eldest son.

In accordance with the injunction of the Koran (42;38: 'the way of the Companions of the Prophet to govern their affairs is by counsel'), the *Kanoun Namé* also decreed the establishment of a system of central conciliar administration which, though overhauled during the reign of Suleiman the Magnificent, remained virtually unaltered for several centuries. Four was a mystic number in Moslem theology: accordingly, the principal officers of state were the Grand Vizier; the *Kazi-Asker*, or Judge Advocate; the *Defterdar*, or Minister of Finance; and the *Nichandji*, or Secretary of State. The Grand Vizier was much the most powerful, combining the administrative and secretarial functions of a European chancellor with powers of detailed oversight and intervention in the spheres of foreign policy and military organization. Grand Viziers were also expected to lead armies in the field. Each of these officials was personally nominated by the sultan and served only during his pleasure.

It would be naïve to suppose that administrative efficiency alone governed appointments to the highest posts. Faction played a large part; the Grand Vizier Rustem Pasha, for instance, who held office, save for one brief interval of disgrace, from 1544 to his death in 1561, was the central figure in a palace faction which included Khurrem, the favourite consort of Suleiman, her daughter – and Rustem's wife – the Princess Mihrumah, and his brother Sinan Pasha, who was *kapudan* (high admiral) of the fleet from 1550-4.

In provincial government no distinction was drawn between civil and military authority. The administration of large cities like Damascus or great provinces like Egypt was entrusted to pashas, this being a title, not an office, indicating that its holder had been admitted to the highest ruling circle of the empire and membership of the *Divan*, or State Council. These officials were regularly transferred from one post to another, to prevent them from developing local loyalties or building personal systems of patronage and power. Practice was somewhat different in the conquered territories of

26, 27 The seraglio, or harem, ceremoniously regulated by slave officials such as the black eunuch (right) played an increasingly significant role in Ottoman court politics. Suleiman's Circassian consort Khurrem (above), conspired to secure the succession for her sons

Balkan Europe which most nearly concern us, where senior officials normally retained office for long periods of time. European Turkey was considered to be an administrative unity called the *Eyalet* of Rumeli, whose supreme governor was the *Beglerbeg*; during the 1540s two new Hungarian *beglerbegliks* were created, with their capitals at Buda and Temesvar. The area was subdivided during the fifteenth century into *sanjaks*, most of which were reorganized during the sixteenth century in groups of two or three into twenty-four *pashaliks*, governed, as their name implies, by officers of the rank of pasha, who were, however, in the western Balkans, as in other frontier regions of the empire, entitled *begs*. These officials were granted special fiefs called *tschiftliks* for the maintenance of their bodyguard and secretariat.

In certain geographical locations and in certain spheres of administration the Ottomans impinged scarcely at all on the life of the

28, 29 A *beglerbeg* in the regalia of his office (left). The *élite* groups in the administration and armed forces of the Ottoman empire in Europe were generally slaves recruited from the child tribute of Christian provinces. The youth in the conical hat (right), wearing the uniform of one of the palace schools, is being prepared for service as a janissary

rayas, the non-Moslem subjects of the sultan. The great Orthodox monasteries in Greece and Macedonia, for example, many of which were landed proprietors on an immense scale, retained full rights of administration over their peasants and estates, as they had done under the Byzantine empire. In some mountainous and coastal areas of Greece, free villages (*kefalochoria*) remained undisturbed under the rule of their own elders, on condition that they paid taxes or furnished recruits (*galiondjis*) for the Ottoman navy. Throughout the Balkans certain fields of legal administration – particularly the important sphere of family law – were consigned entirely to the resident Greek Orthodox clergy under their regional patriarchs. Outside very large and strategically significant towns like Belgrade, which each had a resident administration and constituted an island of effective occupation, the *begs* and their attendants governed peripatetically, moving from fortress to fortress and living as a garrison in an alien land. When the central government in Constantinople wished to execute some important task, such as the compilation of a census, a registration of property or the collection of *devshirme*, the child tribute of the Balkans for recruitment into the army or administration, officials of the royal slave household were dispatched from the capital armed with special warrants and powers.

The creation of this administrative apparatus reflected a masterful and deliberate manipulation by Turkish statesmen of elementary social forces. As was stressed in the first chapter, the origins of the Ottoman state lay in the predatory operations of a nomadic warband which was always on the move and perpetually poised for attack: a literal instrument of conquest. These circumstances generated two governing principles of Ottoman social evolution. The first was the primacy of military arrangements and organization. The second was the necessity for fluidity, the compulsion, operative on any group whose sole collective purpose is robbery and conquest, to borrow, absorb and adapt ideas, social practices and institutions in order to keep contact with and control over the peoples which it incorporates and exploits. As the modern Turkish sociologist, Ziya Gökalp (1876–1924), observed:

45

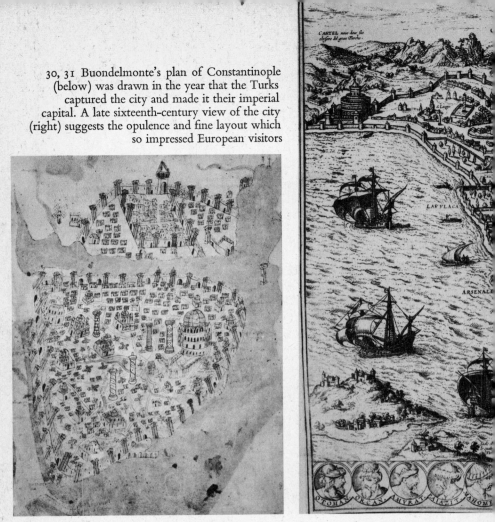

30, 31 Buondelmonte's plan of Constantinople (below) was drawn in the year that the Turks captured the city and made it their imperial capital. A late sixteenth-century view of the city (right) suggests the opulence and fine layout which so impressed European visitors

When the Ottoman pattern took an imperialistic course . . . the Ottoman class were the ruling cosmopolitans . . . the civilization of the Ottomans was a mixture of institutions borrowed from the Turkish, Persian and Arab cultures, from the religion of Islam, from the Eastern and, more recently, Western civilizations.

The central problem which confronted the Ottoman sultans and their advisers after the capture of Constantinople had assured them of an imperial destiny was that of harnessing and bridling, without

stifling or repressing, the military energies and enthusiastic plunder-expectations of an oriental horde by the creation of a state which was settled at its centre but expansive and aggressive at its periphery. A good index of the success with which they achieved this difficult synthesis of fundamentally contradictory social processes is provided by noting the coincidence of the spectacular sixteenth-century conquests to be discussed in the next chapter with the very rapid growth of Constantinople as an imperial capital, from a population of less than 100,000 in 1453 to something between 500,000 and 800,000 – far larger than any contemporary European city – in 1600.

The *ghazi* warriors who provided the original cutting edge of Ottoman expansion were land-hungry freebooters of diverse origins. An increase in the size of this group was essential if the Ottoman state was to continue expanding. The *timar* system provided an economic basis for a numerous class of such *sipahis*, whose obedience was ensured by institutionalizing denial of the hereditary principle in the Ottoman law of feudal land-holding, and whose appetite for warfare was stimulated by the enticing prospect of fresh plunder perpetually available across the frontiers of the empire. According to the Venetian ambassador, Marcantonio Barbaro, there were 80,000 *sipahis* in European Turkey in 1573 and 50,000 in the Asiatic provinces, together with 15,000 *sipahis* 'of the Porte', household cavalry who were paid by the treasury and did not receive *timars*. The *sipahis* remained an unruly class, militarily valuable but politically untrustworthy, whose turbulence it was necessary to balance and control by increasing the numbers and improving the efficiency of public administrators and by establishing a body of household infantry whose effectiveness on campaign and loyalty to the sultan were beyond question. It was in response to these requirements that the Ottomans of the fifteenth and sixteenth centuries developed slavery as a fundamental social institution; organizing by

32, 33, 34, 35 *Sipahis*, hungry for booty and promotion, thronged to the encampments such as that in Georgia (opposite) which ringed the frontiers of the Ottoman empire and provided the forward bases for further aggression. *Sipahis* (below centre) formed the feudal military caste of the empire. *Azapis*, or common foot soldiers (left), mostly recruited from the Anatolian peasantry, were supplemented by allied units, typified by the Moorish infantryman (right)

36 Entire captive families were put up for sale before exacting customers in the slave market at Constantinople

this means a supply of obedient and talented soldiers and administrators on a scale suited to the demands of a great imperialist power.

The Dutchman Rycaut wrote in the seventeenth century:

> If a man seriously consider the whole composition of the Turkish Court he will find it to be a prison and banniard of slaves, differing from that where the galley slaves are immured only by the ornaments and glittering outside.

Edward Gibbon in the eighteenth century was less disapproving but equally emphatic when he wrote – with some exaggeration:

> In the vigorous age of the Ottoman government, the Turks were themselves excluded from all civil and military honours; and a servile class, an artificial people, was raised by the discipline of education to obey, to conquer, and to command.

The role of slavery in the Ottoman system requires special analysis, for, as these quotations reveal, the inhumanity of slave-raiding together with traditional European antipathy to the Turks has tended to obscure historians' understanding of this phenomenon.

37 Huge sums were expended by the notables of Constantinople in assembling 'impressive entourages of slave bodyguards and attendants ▶

Turkish slavery did not in the least resemble the slavery which Europeans imposed upon field workers in the plantations of the New World in the course of the sixteenth century; nor was it in most cases as onerous as the serfdom which was inflicted upon the peasant class of eastern Europe during the same period. The comparatively mild character of Turkish slavery derived from the fact that slaves were not valued primarily for the economic utility of their labour. They were used instead to satisfy the ambition of Ottoman notables (often slaves themselves) to accumulate a large household of attendants as a public expression of their personal wealth and power. Competitive conspicuous display of enormous slave trains was a characteristic feature of the social life of Constantinople. When the Grand Vizier Rustem Pasha died in 1561 it was recorded that his household included 1,700 slaves; that of the sixteenth-century sultans, excluding the janissaries and the ruler's personal bodyguard, contained between 20,000 and 25,000. Since a numerous and loyal slave household helped to ensure a great man's personal safety, precautionary considerations impelled Turkish magnates to treat their slaves with at least a modicum of consideration.

Slaves in Ottoman society were therefore primarily personal bodyguards and servants. Galley slaves were the only important exception to this rule; and the emphasis laid on their sufferings in contemporary European travellers' accounts of Ottoman life is an unintentional testimony to the generally easy circumstances which other slaves enjoyed. Slave women played the role of concubines and mothered the heirs of the Ottoman ruling class. The sultan himself was almost always the son of a slave mother. Great dignitaries directed the affairs of the empire through the agency of their slave households. The royal slave-family administered the secular side of the sultan's government and furnished the corps d'élite of his army. All this is far removed from our normal assumptions about what enslavement implies. The slave population of the barracks, arsenals, chancellories and palaces of Constantinople were utterly different from the brutalized Negro slave-hands of the Americas, who constitute the European archetype of an enslaved people.

Islam sanctioned slavery so long as the enslaved populations were not already Moslem or had not formally submitted to the sovereignty of a Moslem ruler by payment of the prescribed poll-tax. On every frontier against the Christian world Ottoman or allied raiding parties were perpetually searching for slaves. Since the supply was not always adequate even to meet the demands of the imperial household, the Turks adopted the policy of enslaving selected young men from inside the Ottoman borders. In the early fifteenth century the sultans began to take tribute of male children between the ages of six and fifteen from the wild and remote villages of Greece and the western Balkans, where money taxes were difficult to collect. This regulated enslavement kept the royal household well staffed, but did nothing to satisfy the insistent demand of lesser dignitaries for recruits to their own households. The appetite of the slave market in Constantinople remained insatiable.

Mediterranean pirates and frontier fighters in Danubian Europe did something to meet this demand; but Ottoman slave markets found their principal source of supply in the Pontic hinterland. In this region a warlike population of slave raiders, the Crimean Tartars, already existed in close juxtaposition to an experienced mercantile community in the ports of the Black Sea. These merchants and Tartars were long accustomed to cooperating with each other. During the period of Genoese dominion, Tartar caravan leaders collected goods from the countryside and delivered them to the merchants of Caffa and other coastal towns, who took over responsibility at the water's edge. No readjustment of this pattern was required when the goods in transit ceased to be sacks of grain and became human beings. Tartar transportation problems, indeed, were very greatly simplified; for this merchandise could and did walk long distances to market.

Nowhere else on the margins of the Ottoman empire did such a combination of circumstances prevail. In Hungary, for example, slave raiding never attained similar importance for want of a marketing organization to deliver the captives to urban centres; while local Ottoman officials, for whom the serfs attached to their estates already performed all necessary services, had only limited uses for slaves. From Pontic Europe, on the contrary, the ravenous urban markets of the Ottoman world were easily available via Caffa. Once this was evident to all parties, Tartar slave raids became an annual enterprise which was suspended only in very unusual political circumstances or at times when outbreaks of plague in the country districts made the risks prohibitive. Polish records of Tartar slave raids into the Ukraine in the sixty years from 1474 to 1534 refer to thirty-seven separate expeditions, some of which were continuous over several years. Between 1482 and 1512 only five years passed without a recorded raid; and there is no reason to believe that this documentation is complete or takes notice of any but large-scale operations.

The inhumanity and social destructiveness of systematic slavery need no emphasis. Yet individual captives who survived the hardships of transportation to urban slave markets entered a rich and often extremely rewarding new world. A slave career among the Turks offered extensive opportunities to these enforced migrants from isolated and poverty-stricken villages. Slaves of the royal household were the wealthiest and most powerful men of the empire; they commanded Ottoman armies, governed the provinces and framed the policy of the state. Ascent to the pinnacle of the Ottoman power-structure was, of course, unusual; yet the life of even the humblest slave in a great household was in most respects preferable to the remembered privations and monotony of village existence. Indignity and brutality sometimes occurred between master and man – but this was no less true of the social life of the villages from which the slaves had come. Nostalgia for violently broken personal and family ties makes an appearance in some cycles of Ukrainian folk songs; but in general such evidence as we have suggests that the wider opportunities of the new life were ample compensation for the loss of psychological security.

The best proof of the magnetic influence exercised by Ottoman society over the slaves who were pressed into its service was the regularity with which the captives accepted Islam. Physical force was not in question; nor was there normally any energetic proselytism. The pressures of social circumstance and expectation sufficed to persuade almost all slaves to conform, at least outwardly, to Moslem piety. This was possible without expressly repudiating the (sometimes only vaguely) Christian practices of their village past. Islam assigned an honourable, if subordinate, place to Christianity by recognizing it as a forerunner of the Prophet's final revelation of the divine will and purpose. Christians therefore enjoyed a regulated, inferior, but legal and well-defined place in Ottoman society. In abandoning their Christian identity, slaves of great Ottoman households were in effect only admitting that their new life had enhanced or superseded earlier, parochial religious experience. Heterodox Moslem tradition made such a view particularly plausible. Dervish orders like the Bektashi, with whom some branches of the sultan's household had close and special connections, taught that all organized religion – Christianity and Islam alike – represented an imperfect approximation to the truth, which lay in mystic personal communion with God. In accepting Moslem forms of faith a convert from Christianity could easily believe that he was repudiating nothing except the bigotry of his childhood training.

In the fifteenth and sixteenth centuries the energy of the Ottoman empire, the vigour of its bureaucracy and the valour of its armies

38 Members of a dervish order dancing in religious frenzy

therefore depended on massive enslavement of peasant populations drawn from the fringes of the territory under Ottoman control. Simple village boys who entered the special academies of Constantinople, the schools of the Pages, of the Janissaries and of the Palace, were systematically trained for the tasks of defending, extending and governing one of the world's great empires on behalf of a monarch who was himself half slave. A career wide open to talent projected a succession of outstandingly able men to the summit of power. So long as authority was monopolized by bureaucrats who remembered their childhood in remote Balkan or Pontic villages, the bias of official action – and inaction – usually included some sympathy for peasant populations. The high officials of the empire tended to enforce strict legal limitations on the goods and services which a Moslem landholder could demand from the tenants living on his estates. A permanent tension resulted between the sultan's slave officials and Moslem cavalry fief holders; but it was from this balance that both the personal power of the sultan and the general welfare of the Balkan populations under his administration proceeded. So long as this creative tension was maintained, the Ottoman imperial system remained formidable in contrast to the comparatively slender population resources, crude techniques and anarchic political traditions inherited by the rulers of the marcher states of eastern Europe. The entire military strength of the Ottoman empire could be mobilized for field operations with no danger of revolt in the rear, while the field army itself was disciplined and obedient to a single imperial will.

The military flower of this slave system was the janissary corps of infantry archers which was formed in 1438 and recruited through most of the fifteenth and sixteenth centuries from the child tribute of the western Balkans. Janissary detachments were stationed in all the major garrison towns of the empire, though the Constantinople corps was the most numerous and efficient. This numbered about 12,000 during the reign of Suleiman the Magnificent. By 1683 it was five or six times as large – but by this period both the composition and the efficiency of the janissaries had become seriously adulterated.

39, 40 Two impressions by sixteenth-century Turkish artists of Suleiman the Magnificent's victory over the Hungarian army at Mohacs in 1526. Note, to the right of the miniature (below), the sultan backed by a phalanx of tall-hatted janissaries. This was the human barrier against which the Hungarian cavalry dashed itself to pieces

41, 42, 43 A janissary going into battle (left). The discipline and bravery of these household infantry made them the most formidable component of sixteenth-century Turkish armies. Right, Warrior's Rest: a scene of camp life; and (far right) a Turkish prostitute

During the fifteenth and through most of the sixteenth century their discipline and loyalty to the sultan were reinforced by a strict prohibition of marriage; but occasional exceptions were permitted during the last years of Suleiman's reign, and the rule was entirely relaxed during the reign of Selim II (1556–74). The janissaries were equipped with hand guns about 1500. Their steadiness and cohesion in close-quarter fighting and skill with these weapons routed the Mamaluke armies and hastened the Ottoman conquest of Syria and Egypt during 1516–17, and dispersed the last desperate assault of the Christian cavalry at the crucial battle of Mohacs which delivered the Hungarian kingdom to Suleiman in 1526.

The role of slavery in the Ottoman system was not the only important difference between the structure of the Ottoman empire and that of the eastern and central European monarchies on which it preyed during the fifteenth and sixteenth centuries. Another was the contrast between the stress laid in each on the hereditary principle. This principle remained weak in Ottoman society; a magnate class comparable to the assertive aristocracies of Renaissance and

Reformation Europe did not exist on Turkish soil. The effectiveness of Ottoman government was directly related to the fact that no serious check was placed on the exercise of the personal authority of the sultan by the presence and activity of a rooted territorial aristocracy.

Even among free-born Moslem fighting men pride of descent and strong family loyalties were rare. Most of them were social upstarts, arrived from nowhere, sons of slaves and concubines who so far outranked their ancestors as to be totally uninterested in them. Turkish domestic life and sexual manners were those of an army encamped. Once the summer campaign was ended Ottoman warriors were ready enough to take as wives and concubines whatever attractive women happened to be available. But when the command came to report for the new campaigning season they left both women and offspring to fend for themselves until they returned in the autumn – or perhaps failed to return, depending on the chances of war, the availability of a cosier billet or the command of some military superior.

Projected upon society as a whole, the comparative weakness of both family ties and the hereditary principle among the governing classes of the empire meant that resistance to the encroachments of bureaucratic centralized government was far less vigorous in the Ottoman world than in any contemporary Christian society. The social magnetism of Constantinople and the other great towns and the inheritance by the Ottomans of Byzantine legal and political traditions worked powerfully in the same direction, strengthening the position of the sultan against Moslem landholders who were the mainstay of his armies but also his potential opponents.

Until the mid-sixteenth century, therefore, the free-born fighting men who entered the sultan's service tended to detach themselves from all past anchorages almost as completely as the slaves of the royal household who commanded the cavalry in the field. Perpetual campaigning involved heavy human losses, not only in battle but also from the accidents and disease which were unavoidable in the primitive and insalubrious conditions of frontier warfare. The result was a very rapid turnover of personnel and possessions. So long as the empire continued to expand, conquest of each new province occasioned a disturbance of the property-holding system as its lands were shared out among the victors. Most Turkish warriors shifted winter quarters too frequently to allow them to put down roots or to feel that a particular estate was their personal and permanent possession rather than a convenient source of food, income and services during a limited period of military inactivity. With land in the possession of such a class, local resistance to administrative centralization was notably weaker than in European societies, where a formidable aristocracy, firmly attached to their family acres, stubbornly resisted any innovation proposed by despised bureaucrats in the service of an ambitious monarch. The only exception to this rule in the European provinces of the Ottoman empire was in Bosnia, where the local territorial aristocracy was converted *en masse* to Islam during the fifteenth century. The Sacred Law did not allow expropriation of the lands of true believers; and in Bosnia the power of the monarchy was therefore circumscribed in much the same fashion as prevailed universally throughout Christian Europe.

60

44 The hazards of incessant frontier warfare took a heavy toll of military manpower. This detail from a Turkish miniature of 1582 shows janissaries drowning while fording a river ▶

The contrast between the Ottoman and Christian systems of land tenure was also important from the peasants' point of view. The Turkish warrior was usually absent from his estates for half the year and could leave no effective representative behind him when his return was always a matter of uncertainty; this left large scope for the development of village autonomy. The aristocracy of Christian Europe, by contrast, attached to particular locations by family tradition, had long since worked their way into the fabric of village life, leaving small opportunity for peasants to manage

their own affairs. Occasional extreme brutality and violent interruption of routine was the price which villagers in the Ottoman empire paid for their comparative freedom of action. This occurred whenever an overlord or intruder unexpectedly intervened to demand some service or supply of goods above and beyond the relatively light obligations imposed by fiat of the sultan. Such sporadic violence disfigured but did not destroy the normal autonomy of village life under the Turks.

The Ottoman empire of the fifteenth and sixteenth centuries was therefore dependent upon conservation of a comparatively lightly burdened peasantry in the central regions of the state, coupled with determined and systematic predation upon similar communities lying just beyond the territorial limits of Turkish administration. The centre could sustain organized military power on a grand scale only by preying upon peripheral communities, while maintaining a secure home base where restriction upon exploitation of the lower orders of society assured a high degree of stability. The contrived and radical institutional forms of recruitment and conversion in the Ottoman world, so surprising and so repugnant to Europeans, were in fact unusually drastic and effective devices for guaranteeing the continued strength and prosperity of the metropolitan centre.

The religious gulf between Christianity and Islam widened the divergence between the Ottoman empire and European states. For a brief period during the fifteenth century this gulf did not appear unbridgeable; the Turks were busily appropriating elements of the Byzantine heritage, and echoes of the secularism of the Italian Renaissance attracted equally favourable attention at the court of the king of Hungary and in the Constantinople of Mohammed the Conqueror. But the sixteenth century brought a sharp revulsion from the latitudinarianism which was current in advanced circles during the fifteenth. Both Christianity and Islam encapsulated themselves in a revived and intolerant orthodoxy whose champions were increasingly impervious to external stimuli. The circumstances which provoked this reaction were similar on each side of the religious dividing line. The outbreak of Shi'a rebellion in eastern Anatolia in 1514 anticipated and in some respects paralleled the wave of religious revolt which was raised by Martin Luther in Germany and north-western Europe in the years after 1517.

The seventy-two contending sects which traditional Moslem scholarship somewhat arbitrarily discerned within the community of the faithful were divided by the ancient issue of the legitimacy of the succession to the Prophet into two main groups: the Shi'a, who held that the succession rightfully descended only through Mohammed's son-in-law Ali; and the Sunni, who recognized the legitimacy of Abu Bakr, Omar and Othman – sometime associates of Mohammed, who historically were the effective inheritors of his authority – and their successors in the caliphate. This basic division of allegiance was complicated by the rise and proliferation from the eighth century onwards of mystical (Sufi) orders, brotherhoods and congregations who 'walked familiarly with God' and objected to the encasement of the Moslem faith in an armour of orthodox learning and law. It was blurred still further by the emergence of heterodox religious groups which were receptive to Shi'a influences while remaining Sunni in the sense of admitting the legitimacy of the first three caliphs. Confusion was compounded by the fact that though in most areas the Shi'a remained a more or less persecuted minority, their practice of simulating Sunni orthodoxy while revealing hidden truths only to trusted initiates spread a wide variety of clandestine Shi'a groups throughout the Moslem world. On this basis a restless balance between the sects of Islam had long prevailed, subject to recurrent local disturbance whenever a particularly holy man won a strong following or some zealot arose to proclaim the damnation of all who differed from his theological principles.

The frequently precarious grasp on power of the Turkish war-lords who divided and disputed control over the peoples of Islam after the eleventh century contributed to the maintenance of this balance, since few rulers cared or dared to run the risk of rebellion by insisting too strenuously upon religious conformity. The Ottoman state was no exception to this rule; for though the sultans adopted a policy of support for Sunni orthodoxy, declaring it to be the official religion of the empire during the fifteenth century, they never entirely broke off relations with the heterodox dervish

45 The emergence of an aggressive Shi'a monarchy in Persia under the leadership of Shah Ismail Safavi (left), who ruled from 1500 to 1523, divided the Moslem Middle East in much the same way as the contemporary Protestant Reformation divided Christian Europe

46 Ismail Safavi (on horse with gilded armour) in battle against the king of Shirvan Persia (1500). This was the first of the campaigns leading to the formation of the Safavid empire. Ismail's military triumphs involved the Turks with a protracted 'Persian problem' which frequently reduced the effectiveness of their offensives in Europe during the sixteenth and earlier seventeenth centuries ▶

communities whose religious enthusiasm had contributed so greatly to early Ottoman expansion.

The religious and political equilibrium of Islam was drastically disturbed in 1499 when a fanatical Shi'a sect whose homeland lay near the southern shores of the Caspian Sea began to extend its influence and to win a series of great military victories. Beginning with a scattering of fervent followers, the leader of the sect, Ismail Safavi, rapidly built up a formidable army. In 1500 he captured Tabriz and crowned himself shah. By 1506 the entire Iranian plateau was united under the new conqueror; and in 1508 he took Baghdad and most of Iraq. This was the basis of a powerful new Persian monarchy.

Ismail persecuted all Sunni Moslems and supported a vigorous Shi'a propaganda beyond the frontiers of his kingdom. His victories encouraged numerous Shi'a sympathizers to come out into the open in many parts of the Moslem world, especially in eastern Anatolia,

دوکوه ازدوشکرنمود ک

بجنبید کوه وبلرزید

ز خولان هنران ابن سیله   درمد بهفت اسمان

where they presented a threat which the Ottoman sultan could not overlook. In 1514 a widespread Shi'a revolt against the Ottomans broke out in Anatolia, suppression of which required full-scale mobilization of the Turkish army. After quelling the heretics at home, the Ottoman forces advanced eastwards against the source of the infection itself. At the battle of Tchaldiran (1514) Turkish artillery prevailed against Safavi fanaticism; but the sultan was compelled to withdraw without destroying the basis of Ismail's power. Throughout the remainder of the sixteenth century the Safavi empire remained a profoundly disturbing force in the Moslem world, dedicated to the defence and propagation of Shi'a doctrines. This policy implied a normal state of hostility with the Ottoman empire, punctuated only briefly by periods of truce; no lasting peace was concluded until 1639.

After their failure to overthrow the Persian empire in 1514, the Ottomans were soon forced to take further military action to forestall an incipient alliance between Ismail and the Mamaluke ruler of Egypt and Syria. Sultan Selim I conquered the Mamaluke kingdom in a single campaign (1516–17) thanks to the discipline of the janissaries and to the same artillery superiority which he had enjoyed against the Persians. His victory also gave the Ottomans control over the important holy cities of Mecca and Medina, which had long been dependencies of the Mamalukes.

From his newly acquired bases in Egypt Selim also began to extend his power over the coastal cities of North Africa in an attempt to limit the expansion of a second insurgent Shi'a monarchy, that of the Sa'di Sharifs of Morocco. By 1511 the Sharifs had organized a powerful state among the tribal and urban peoples of the Moslem far-west on the strength of a religious propaganda similar to that which had achieved such dramatic success in Persia and Iraq. It was the urgent necessity of checking this development which first brought Ottoman naval squadrons into action off the Algerian coast – thus incidentally provoking the long sixteenth-century naval wars with Spain. In North Africa, however, common hostility to the Iberian Christians prevented any direct clash between the Ottoman and Moroccan states.

47 A late sixteenth-century European impression of hostilities between the Ottoman and Persian empires in 1514. In many of its details this woodcut has been
transposed into a central European context

Inside their own dominions it became the settled policy of the
sixteenth-century Ottoman sultans to suppress heresy without taking
the risk of attempting to uproot it altogether. Heterodox dervish
orders were too closely interwoven with the fabric of the Ottoman
state to be frontally attacked. The janissaries, for example, could be
counted upon to defend their spiritual advisers, the Bektashi dervishes; and other dervish orders were similarly affiliated with urban
gilds in Constantinople and with regional communities in Anatolia.
After the revolt and massacres of 1514 most Shiʻa sympathizers in
Ottoman territory reverted to their traditional ruse of outward
conformity to Sunni practices. Serious resistance was confined to
outlying areas; a rising, spurred on by dervishes, among the Tur-
coman tribes of Karaman and the Taurus mountains broke out in
1526 and took two years to suppress. Apart from this necessary show

of military strength in remote provinces the sultans contented themselves with administrative precautions. Suleiman strengthened the hierarchical organization of the *ulema* of the empire, subsidized Sunni educational institutions and generally put the weight of his government behind a strictly-conceived Sunnite orthodoxy. As a result of these measures the heterodox (often crypto-Shi'a) doctrines of the dervishes found less and less public expression. Their teachings traditionally emphasized the resemblances between Islam and Christianity and provided an effective bridge between them. The gap between the two religious communities in the empire therefore tended to widen. It was widened still further when the Ottoman sultans of the sixteenth century were obliged to magnify their role as standard bearers of the *Jihad* in order to mobilize enthusiasm among their Moslem subjects for a long series of wars against Europeans in the Mediterranean and eastern Europe.

Suleiman's legislation froze the intellectual life of the Ottoman empire into fixed and complacent patterns. Instead of having to meet challenges to the Sunni version of the Sacred Law on an intellectual plane, Turkish Moslems found it possible, as a result of the measures taken by the Ottoman government, to fall back upon officially approved conformity and occasional persecution when confronted by Shi'a heresy. In the long run this intellectual and moral abdication cost them dearly. Slowly but surely the Turks' studied indifference to any but strictly traditional patternings of the life of the mind was to allow Europe to outstrip the Ottoman world in one region of thought and action after another, without ever provoking any Moslem response. In the short run, however, all the advantages seemed to lie with the Turks. Religious order and discipline on the Moslem side of the frontier contrasted with the riotous confusion of Reformation Europe, where the rival doctrines of Rome, Wittenberg and Geneva clashed with each other and with the radical beliefs of Baptists and Unitarians. Yet the mutual vituperation of the Christian sects stimulated them occasionally to attain a level of intellectual discourse which had no analogue among the Moslems.

In the eyes of contemporary Europeans, especially those who found themselves pitted against Turkish armies and navies in eastern

Europe and the Mediterranean, the Ottoman empire of the fifteenth and sixteenth centuries appeared to be an overpowering and invincible adversary. Yet within the social institutions and processes which powered this triumphant imperial progress, there were latent incoherencies and contradictions which, emerging and sharpening with the passage of time, were eventually to reduce the proud empire to a condition of paralysis and exhaustion.

For all its external pomp and circumstance, in one important respect the empire of the Ottoman sultans remained – indeed had no alternative but to remain – faithful to the purposes of the tatterde-malion raiding party from which it had evolved; it was organized for plundering and it subsisted on plunder. The resources which sustained the growth of Constantinople into a great metropolis

48 Turks on stilts in the snow, Belgrade. The momentum of Ottoman expansion on the European frontier was finally halted by a fatal combination of climate and geography

could only be obtained by raiding across the frontiers. Frontier raiding on the massive scale which had now become necessary was work for great armies. Recruitment of these could be – and was – effected in only two ways. Firstly, fiefs could be distributed in return for military service; but since expropriation of existing Moslem landowners was forbidden by the Sacred Law, land could only be obtained in sufficient quantities by extension of the frontier, that is, by more raiding. Secondly, a slave army could be assembled; but slaves were prizes which could only be won by yet more raiding. The loyalty and enthusiasm of both these military elements depended on the provision of perpetual opportunities for further plunder and upon the presence and obedience of a slave administration; all of which implied more raiding again.

This was a circular system in which everything depended on an inexhaustible supply of slaves, booty and land. Given the comparatively crude and elementary techniques of warfare, transportation, communication and administration available to the Ottomans, which must eventually impose their limitations on operation of the system, it could not perpetuate itself. Yet disengagement from the pursuit of plunder was unthinkable; a retreat behind stable frontiers would lead inevitably to the disintegration of the central authority as a result of its inability to remain in control of the instruments of war and conquest which it had called into existence. Fief-holders would take advantage of prolonged periods of peace to anchor themselves and their families to their estates, impervious to the commands of the central government; while the slave soldiery, deprived of the prospect of plunder, would transfer their loyalty from their master, replacing him by a sultan prepared to cater to their appetites and resume the interrupted sequence of conquest and border raiding. The very real possibility of this last development was made abruptly apparent even to a majestic sultan like Suleiman; three years without war produced a serious disturbance among the janissaries of Constantinople in 1525. And in spite of the military triumphs of 1526, events later in the same decade inexorably underlined the other side of the problem, the technical impossibility of conducting spectacularly successful warfare at very long range.

'Snow from evening until noon next day'; 'much loss of horses and men in swamps'; 'many die of hunger': so run the sultan's official war diaries recording the retreat from Vienna to Belgrade in 1529. The internal logic of this system was self-defeating and self-destructive; it could win great victories, but it could not operate for long.

While the Ottoman empire was, in this sense, doomed by its inability to liberate itself from its origins, in another important respect its prospects were compromised by a precisely opposite tendency: namely, an historical experience which prevented the continued operation of a vital Ottoman tradition. The secret of the success of the earliest Ottomans was their remarkable power of assimilation. The original war-band was not a tribe, whose members were knit together in a pattern of kinship relations which excluded strangers. It was a party of fighting nomads on migration, a voluntary organization under a chosen leader, which anyone could join. As it went from success to success it assimilated captive men and women from the farming settlements it pillaged and recruits from rival marauding groups it defeated in battle; it was joined by wandering dervishes eager for an audience, by renegades and social outcasts from Byzantine territories and by a swarm of peasants uprooted and driven by Mongol invasions from their holdings in Anatolia. In an analogous way all the features which subsequently became characteristic of Ottoman culture were picked up and incorporated *en route*. It was this remarkable assimilative capacity which explains the lightning speed of early Ottoman conquest. The Ottomans did not remain apart from and alien to the peoples whom they conquered; for having no identity themselves beyond that of a fighting force loyal to a particular commander, nothing was alien to them except peace.

All this changed drastically when they were converted to Islam. Conversion implied much more than acceptance of certain theological principles and religious practices. It meant being drawn into the framework of one of the world's great cultures, with its own distinctive patterns of law, social and political organization, artistic endeavour and attitudes to human life and destiny. As a total way of life Islam was extraordinarily rich and diverse, permitting a wide variety of choices and interpretations; but it was also intolerant and exclusive, above all fiercely hostile to those of different faiths. As *The Legacy of Islam* puts it:

> This community is different from any other: it is the chosen, the holy people, to whom is entrusted the furtherance of good and the repression of evil; it is the only seat of justice and faith upon earth, the sole witness for God among the nations, just as the Prophet had been God's witness among the Arabs.

This mattered not at all while the Ottomans were operating entirely within the geographical context of the Moslem world; but during the fourteenth and fifteenth centuries, as their state grew from a fluid frontier emirate into a great empire, it established dominion over very large populations of Christian subjects in south-eastern Europe. At this stage, according to their deepest traditions, it would have been 'natural' for the Ottomans to have adopted the religion of their new subjects. But they were now dedicated to the fanatical and intolerant religion of Islam, and burdened, too, with a mass of Moslem subjects in their Asiatic provinces whose loyalties had to be taken into account. The half-hearted attempts at synthesizing Christianity and Islam, which were fashionable in court circles after Mohammed II captured Constantinople, indicated some awareness of the problem; but a seminar of hired scholars and theologians in the capital could achieve nothing in face of a problem of these dimensions. And, as we have seen, seismic disturbances within the world of Islam itself in the early sixteenth century obliged the sultans to abandon their earlier eclecticism in favour of a particularly rigid and exclusive Sunnite version of the Moslem faith which, while it forbade persecution of Christian subjects, at the same time discouraged any programme of mass conversion of Christian peoples to Islam. This situation was confirmed by the rivalry during the middle years of the sixteenth century between the Ottoman empire and the great powers of Christian Europe: a confrontation which made it essential for the sultans to identify themselves more strenuously than ever as champions of their adopted religion.

The inevitable result was the perpetuation of a wide and un-bridgeable gulf between the Ottomans and their Christian subjects. The Ottoman state was no longer, as in its earliest days, a voluntary association, since Christians could never be admitted into full partnership. Eastern European peasants might at first welcome Ottoman conquest as a relief from the exactions of harsh and un-feeling governing classes; but once the Turks were installed, their religion prevented them from making any permanent or sym-pathetic contacts with their subjects based on mutual confidence or shared beliefs. The *rayas* might tolerate, but would never enthusiastic-ally support, a Moslem government which refused to accept their testimony in law and forbade them to build new churches or to ring church bells. The Ottoman empire in Europe was an impressive administrative artifact; but, held apart by religion, its components could never merge and blend into a coherent whole. Such a system of arbitrarily contrived cohabitation was never likely to grow into an organic society. Any faltering or decline in the efficiency of the military establishment by means of which the Turks policed and defended their European empire was bound to reveal its essential disharmony and impermanence.

Tensions capable of producing such a decline were never far below the surface of Ottoman society. In combination the Moslem *sipahis* and the slave troops and administrators of the royal house-hold formed an irresistible engine of military and political power. Of course it was essential to keep them in equilibrium; but it was from performance of the necessary function of maintaining this balance that the sultanate derived its overwhelming authority. The source of danger lay not in the existence of such a balance *per se*, but in the fact that it was heavily weighted in favour of the slave household. During the reign of Suleiman it was almost impossible for a free-born Moslem, whatever his qualifications, to reach a position of eminence either in the army or in the bureaucracy. The highest posts were reserved for the *kullar*, the enslaved 'men of the sultan', while the feudal class of the empire, warriors of Turkish descent, many of whom were proud of their exertions in Ottoman service, were excluded from privilege and power. Careers open to talent were all very well; but this Moslem Turkish empire threatened to develop into a system where talent was rewarded only if one was neither a born Moslem nor a Turk. Natural and increasing resentment among the *sipahis* was reinforced by adventitious factors, particularly the economic inflation which was experienced by the Ottoman empire in common with all other Mediterranean societies during the second half of the sixteenth century. Inflation afforded considerable opportunities for gain to holders of public office, while adversely affecting those who subsisted on the fixed incomes of landed estates; but the essential problem stemmed from the imperfect balance of social forces in the imperial machinery of war and government. The events of the 1550s, when the three sons of Suleiman were jockeying for the succession, testified to its seriousness. All three built up formidable private armies by promising disaffected *sipahis* promotion to important posts in the royal household once their leader had ascended the throne. In some cases *sipahis* were formally invested with the status of janissaries as a guarantee of the intention to admit them to the privileged ranks of the *kullar*. Only when two of the ambitious princes had been executed was peace restored; and a less imperious sultan than Suleiman would probably have lost control of the situation altogether.

Even during its period of maximum success, therefore, the Ottoman military and administrative system was displaying symptoms of severe internal strain. The flaws thus revealed were bound to reassert themselves once the furious career of sixteenth-century conquest ground to an inevitable halt and power passed to sultans and Grand Viziers of merely ordinary capacity.

For the Ottoman empire, as a member of the family of Islamic peoples, the Shi'a-Sunni controversy constituted the essential feature of its historical experience during the sixteenth and seventeenth centuries; by comparison the collision with Europe remained marginal. Alignment with the cause of Sunnite orthodoxy must have seemed to the Ottoman sultans a grave and necessary decision of state whereby a restless and fluid society was submitted to the discipline of a conservative system of Moslem instruction and belief. Contrasting the order which prevailed in their own dominions with

74

the confusions of Reformation Europe, Ottoman statesmen could feel that they had successfully weathered the religious crisis which threatened the dissolution of their society during the early sixteenth century. The result was sublime smugness vis-à-vis both heretics and unbelievers, and an unflinching conservatism bent upon discarding all novelties. Shackled to ancient formulae, the minds of Moslems in the Ottoman empire increasingly neglected those elements in the intellectual heritage of Islam which might have enabled them to keep pace with the extraordinary series of cultural and economic revolutions which were about to take place in Europe. Something akin to the spirit of the Italian Renaissance had been fitfully abroad at the court of Mohammed the Conqueror; but Selim the Grim and Suleiman the Magnificent undertook to suppress dangerous thoughts throughout their dominions. They were so successful that no revival of the enquiring, innovating spirit which, in Europe, gave birth to modern literature and science ever occurred in the Ottoman empire. Having balked at meeting the intellectual challenge of heresy by anything more than strident reaffirmation of the past, a paralyzing precedent inhibited any more constructive response to subsequent challenges of the same sort. Pious and educated Sunni Moslems came to feel that uncritical acceptance of religious truth was the only safe and convenient intellectual posture. But in the absence of controversy, intellectual vigour rapidly faded away; and the *ulema* became less and less perfect masters even of their own intellectual inheritance. This stagnation of ideas was a high price to pay for the suppression of heresy; in it lay the central failure of Islam in modern times.

The social structure of the Islamic world contributed powerfully to this outcome. New notions could not hope to find congenial soil in a state composed of a small class of officials and soldiers raised far above a tax-burdened peasantry; and the servility of townsmen towards officials and landlords had been a persistent feature of Middle Eastern society since the second millennium B C. In the short run the Ottoman empire, by the very splendour of its imperial organization, reinforced this social pattern. But in the long run the Ottoman response to the Shi'a-Sunni controversy contributed to its eventual disruption. By their vigorous support of Sunni orthodoxy the Ottoman sultans opened a dangerous gap between the ruling caste and the common classes of the towns. From the sixteenth century onwards artisans and tradesmen became more and more imbued with vulgar superstition and thaumaturgy. A ponderous and unimaginative Sunnite establishment therefore confronted town populations which were prone to increasingly febrile religious enthusiasms. Alienated by definition from their Christian subjects, and merely tolerated by the Moslem peasantry whose labours sustained the state, the Ottomans were now becoming remote and withdrawn from the urban masses of their empire.

Earlier in this chapter, the Turkish sociologist Ziya Gökalp was quoted in support of the view that the Ottoman imperial system was essentially a constellation of borrowings and adaptations from diverse subject and limitrophic cultures. His final verdict reads: 'These institutions were never really integrated and never produced a harmonious system.' One is drawn back to Gibbon's phrase about the Ottoman ruling class: 'an artificial people'. The empire was a reflection of their energy and intelligence, but also of their lack of generous and creative social purpose. An impressive instrument of war and administration when expertly manipulated, it exhibited almost no capacity for independent development. It was an assemblage of ingenious devices; and sometimes, as Gökalp argued, ingenuity was carried to a point where the results cancelled each other out. Thus the hierarchy of mosque schools (*medrese*), which functioned under the supervision of the *ulema*, initiated Turkish students into traditional cosmopolitan Moslem high culture; at the same time elements of ancient Turkish customary law, embedded in the secular legislation of the Ottomans, were being taught to European slave boys in the palace schools. 'When the *medrese* was transforming the Turks into non-Turks, these institutions were transforming non-Turks into Turks.' Then, as now, it seems, educators were at continuous cross-purposes about the social function of education.

III   THE WARS AGAINST THE WEST: 1520–81

The accession of Suleiman the Magnificent to the Ottoman throne in 1520 was the prelude to major assaults in the Balkans and the Mediterranean. The year 1581, marking the conclusion of hostilities between the Turks and the Holy League of Spain and the Papacy, provides a convenient terminal date. Already in 1577 the Ottomans had turned eastwards to undertake a long war against Persia. The interests of Spain, the principal western protagonist, were simultaneously transferring to the Atlantic; the Netherlands revolt reached a climax with the Spanish sack of Antwerp in 1576, Portugal was annexed in 1580 and war declared against England in 1585. This dispersion of interests temporarily removed both the Balkan and Mediterranean theatres from the mainstream of history.

The sixteenth-century Ottoman wars against the West provide a record of systematic plundering on a grand scale. From the point of their first entrance into history as a nomadic war-band, the Ottomans were carried from one triumph to the next by a ruthless dedication to conquest and predation. Even when the empire became anchored to Constantinople, it was sustained by the booty – the manpower as well as the land, goods and resources – of the borderlands. The perpetual search, in Gibbon's phrase, for 'new enemies and new subjects' was not a policy, weighed against alternatives; it was a law of life, the principle which animated what had now become a large and complex society.

Appetite for plunder dictated much of the detail as well as the strategy of the conflict. The intervals between the great confrontations, even periods of formal truce, found corsairs and border raiders from both sides ceaselessly at work. Only winter interrupted the activities of those for whom robbery was a way of life. Such operations ranged from the depredations of the small bandit and rustler communities strung out in mutual opposition along the religious frontier in the Balkans to those of the North African corsair societies where piracy was central to the economy of sizable states. The dangerously exposed maritime republics of the Adriatic, Venice and Ragusa, suffered particularly severe losses from both Christian and Moslem pirates throughout the sixteenth and well into the seventeenth centuries. At the height of the Turkish offensive during the 1550s and 1560s even the coasts of metropolitan Spain were regularly attacked by Algerian and Moroccan pirates who found willing confederates among the repressed moriscos of Granada.

The pattern of events was always influenced, and sometimes determined, by distractions which prevented the Ottoman sultans on the one hand and the Habsburgs, the principal European champions, on the other from achieving a full concentration of power and resources against the racial and religious enemy. The Emperor Charles V never broke free from the shackles of the dynastic struggle against the French monarchy, the religious and political strife in Germany or the problem of binding the American colonies firmly to Spain. His successor, Philip II, faced protracted revolt in the Netherlands, the richest of Spain's overseas possessions, which obliged him to withdraw his best troops from the Mediterranean in 1566–7, at a time when the Turkish failure to take Malta and the death of Suleiman might otherwise have permitted a period of Spanish initiative.

Ottoman rulers laboured under similar difficulties: war against Persia or Persian spheres of influence in Armenia and the Caucasus in 1534–5, 1548 and 1554–5; operations against Portuguese interlopers in the Red Sea and the Arabian Sea in 1537–8 and continuously from the 1550s for more than thirty years; and bitter succession struggles among the sons of Suleiman from 1553 to 1560.

The tides of war seem also to have ebbed and flowed in conformity with secular movements in the economy. If we regard sixteenth-century Europe and Islam as 'families' of similarly structured societies, periods of relative prosperity appear to have produced in each culture a crop of domestic quarrels, wars between neighbours concerning the division of readily accessible spoils. Periods of economic depression, on the other hand, diverted aggressive energies outside the family circle and channelled them into the Crusade or the *Jihad*. For example, the serious economic difficulties experienced by both groups of societies during the 1550s led, on each side, to the temporary settlement of sectarian and dynastic conflicts which had dominated the preceding decades, and produced during the years which followed an intensification of Mediterranean naval warfare and the resumption of the Ottoman drive into Europe along the Danube.

The two prongs of Turkish attack were overland into Hungary and eastern Europe, and by sea against the Christian-held coasts and islands of the Mediterranean.

HUNGARY AND EASTERN EUROPE

The characteristics of the large Hungarian state which emerged during the late Middle Ages were a consequence of its situation at the western terminus of the Eurasian steppe, in an area traversed by rivers (notably the Danube system) and protected by mountain ranges (notably the great arc of the Carpathians). This geographical configuration allowed the nomad, pastoral economy of the steppe to be supplemented in this region by some primitive agriculture, forestry and mining. The development of these alternative sources of wealth produced a settled class of small cultivators and scattered and rudimentary urban populations. These, however, lay always at the mercy of nomadic conquerors enjoying superior mobility and sustained by warlike practices and traditions. The Magyar horsemen who conquered the plains of the middle Danube in the ninth and tenth centuries were quick to grasp the opportunity offered of exploiting resident human beings rather than the flocks and herds which they had brought with them out of Asia; indiscriminate raiding was abandoned in favour of settlement and a subsequent career as magnates profiting from the labour of subject serfs and craftsmen. Such were the origins of the Hungarian aristocracy.

The feudal society and attitudes of the medieval west offered this ruling class of free warriors a cultural model infinitely more attractive and better suited to their purposes than the caesarism and centralization of the Byzantine world. Drawn over several centuries into the ambit of western Christendom, Hungary remained facing the special problems of a 'marcher' state, whose survival depended on providing a barrier against further incursions by nomadic peoples from the east. Only a powerful monarchy was capable of mobilizing and deploying an army equal to the task. The unruly magnates refused to accept the logic of this situation, seeking always to guarantee their local independence by insisting on the traditionally elective character of Hungarian kingship.

Yet, whatever the legal restrictions on his freedom of action, an unscrupulous and energetic ruler, once in office, might exploit his authority or the fears generated by the prospect of invasion to create a mercenary army which could be employed not only as an instrument of national defence, but also as a means of subduing the nobility. This was the achievement of John Hunyadi (regent, 1444–58) and his son Matthias Corvinus (king, 1458–90). After the death of Matthias, the aristocracy, particularly the lesser nobles, who were more apprehensive of royal power than the great magnates who lived and ruled as independent princes on their vast estates, used their electoral influence to extort from his successors, Ladislas (1498–1516) and Lewis (1516–26) of Bohemia, undertakings to disband mercenary forces and respect aristocratic privileges. This deterioration of the position of the crown caused important defections from the constellation of client states, Moravia, Serbia, Moldavia and Wallachia, with which the magnetism of strong monarchy had surrounded the Hungarian kingdom.

49, 50, 51 Matthias Corvinus, Ladislas V and Lewis II, kings of Hungary

52 The cruelty of the Turks, a favourite theme of European propagandists, was fully matched and frequently surpassed by Christian Europeans. Here a red-hot crown is placed on the head of George Dózsa, leader of the Hungarian peasant revolt of 1514; a comrade lies impaled at his feet. Bitter social dissensions prepared the Hungarian kingdom for overthrow by the Turks in 1526

Social and economic tensions fed upon these political differences. Hungarian agriculture was poor and primitive. During the reign of Matthias, the peasants were impoverished by the demands of a monarch grasping for revenues to maintain his professional army and of an aristocracy whose relatively recent emergence from the role of nomad conquerors disposed them to treat their labour force with a measure of cruelty and contempt exceptional even by the harsh standards of the age. The decrease in request for revenue made by the monarchy after 1490 was more than offset by intensified exactions on the part of nobles now liberated from the controls imposed upon them by Matthias Corvinus. A fierce peasant uprising in 1514 was ruthlessly suppressed; and suppressed, significantly, not by royal troops but by a faction of the lesser magnates under John Zapolyai, *voivod* (war lord) of Transylvania, a confessed aspirant to the throne. The Parliament of 1514 enacted legislation which confirmed and increased the miseries of the peasant and, in the same year, Zapolyai's party sponsored the publication of Istvan Verböczy's *Tripartitum opus iuris consuetudinarii inclyti regni Hungariae*, a

81

codification of aristocratic rights and privileges against both the crown and the serfs.

A monarchy crippled by its elective origins; perpetual aristocratic faction fights; massive unrest among a desperate peasantry: such were the characteristics of the Hungarian kingdom when the Ottomans resumed their offensive on the Danube. A divided Hungary lay now in the path of an empire which had harnessed the aggressive instincts and traditions of a nomadic people to the huge resources of Pontic Europe and the Levant.

Succeeding in 1520 to the throne of Selim I, the Grim, conqueror of Syria and Egypt, the new Sultan Suleiman was expected, in accordance with Ottoman practice, to celebrate his succession with a campaign worthy of his father's example. His armies moved against Hungary in the summer of 1521. Belgrade, the great fortress at the confluence of the middle Danube and associated river systems, was the first objective. Diversionary columns struck westwards along the river Sava and eastwards into Transylvania, while an encircling movement severed communications to the north. After a heavy bombardment and repeated assaults, the city fell in August.

53 The Turkish siege of Belgrade, 1521. The Turks employed a fleet of river boats to overcome their transportation problems and to complete the investment of the city

54 Ferdinand I, archduke of Austria, Holy Roman Emperor (1558–64) and Habsburg claimant to the throne of Hungary. Ottoman imperialism in the Balkans was eventually worn down by his stubborn military resistance and opportunistic diplomacy

The line of the middle Danube from Belgrade to Buda now lay open to Turkish attack.

Mediterranean and Egyptian distractions prevented Suleiman from pressing home his advantage until 1526, when he marched into Hungary again. The divisions within Hungarian society now manifested themselves in a fatal combination of recklessness and indecision. The campaigning season was well advanced, the main opposing forces not making contact until the end of August. A strategy of dogged defence might have slowed the already painful pace of Suleiman's offensive and forced him to retreat before the onset of winter. Instead, the Hungarians staked all on a 'set-piece' battle in which the heavy cavalry of the magnates would be launched against the Sultan's huge army. The resulting engagement at Mohacs, in marshy country just east of the Danube, was the greatest of Suleiman's victories. Harried on the flanks by a mobile and numerically superior enemy and ravaged by artillery fire, the charges of the Hungarian cavalry broke against the janissary detachments which formed the core of the Turkish army. The king and many of his magnates were killed and no organized resistance remained to bar Suleiman's advance to Buda. After plundering the city, he withdrew

to Belgrade. Hungary was shattered and the Ottomans now regarded the central provinces of the kingdom as a plunder area subject to the will of the conqueror.

The survivors of the Hungarian aristocracy elected the 'strong man' Zapolyai to the vacant throne in November 1526, but a simultaneous claim was advanced by Archduke Ferdinand of Austria, brother of Emperor Charles V. Ferdinand's candidacy pledged, at least in prospect, the resources of the greatest European dynasty to the recovery of Hungary. Driven from Buda by Habsburg forces, Zapolyai appealed for help to Suleiman, who backed him as the convenient puppet-ruler of a satellite state which would provide both a defensive outpost and a rich source of tribute for the Ottoman empire. In 1529 the Sultan marched up the Danube for the third time to install Zapolyai in Buda and besiege Ferdinand's capital, Vienna. The first aim was soon achieved, but the second ended in

55 View of the Turkish camp surrounding Vienna, 1529. 'Asia begins at the *Landstrasse*' – the road east from Vienna. All the exertions of Suleiman the Magnificent failed to push that frontier further west

56 John Zapolyai, *voivod* of Transylvania and puppet king ('Janos Kral') of Turkish Hungary from 1526 to 1540

57 Continuous bad weather, supply difficulties and well-organized Habsburg resistance compelled the sultan to raise the siege of Vienna after only eighteen days

failure. Even the formidable military capacity of the Ottomans could not compress the march to Vienna and the successful conduct of difficult siege operations within the limits of a single campaigning season. Yet Suleiman did not return empty-handed; most of the old kingdom of Hungary now acknowledged the rule of his vassal Zapolyai.

Ferdinand's refusal to abandon his claims to the Hungarian crown provoked a further Ottoman assault in 1532, in which desperate Austrian resistance prevented the Sultan from obtaining substantial territorial advantage, but only at the cost of exposing Slavonia and Styria to terrible devastation by marauding Turkish armies. By the terms of a truce in the following year, Ferdinand retained the territory which he still held in Hungary but recognized Zapolyai as ruler of the greater part of the kingdom.

The later 1530s were occupied more by Mediterranean than by Balkan operations, though in 1537 an Austrian army, formed to punish persistent border-raiding into Carinthia, was cut to pieces by local Turkish commanders without assistance from Constantinople; and in the following year Suleiman strengthened his administrative grip on the vassal provinces of Bessarabia and Moldavia, thereby ensuring easy movement into the Balkan theatre for his Tartar allies from the Crimea.

On the death of Zapolyai in 1540 Ferdinand revived his claim to the whole kingdom of Hungary. Suleiman therefore decided to incorporate Hungary fully within the confines of the Ottoman empire. Buda was designated as capital of a new *beglerbeglik* in 1541. Campaigns in 1543 and 1544 obtained a number of river fortresses, notably Visegrad and Gran, which dominated the corridor between the Great and Little Alföld. Ferdinand sought and obtained a truce in 1545, followed by a treaty in 1547. He relinquished his claims on all but a small portion of the former Hungarian kingdom over which he still ruled, and agreed to pay tribute to the sultan even for this. The Ottomans' hold on their Hungarian conquests was thus recognized to be unbreakable, at least until a major change occurred in the balance of military power. These conquests were garrisoned rather than colonized by the Turks, who extorted tribute through officials resident in the fortress towns; predation became regularized into a system of government. In areas outside the zones of military settlement many native Hungarian magnates remained in effective control of their estates. The freedom of local action which they enjoyed under Turkish rule made it unlikely that they would, as a class, give a lead in any struggle for 'liberation' from alien oppression. Their fundamental loyalties had already been revealed when they supported Zapolyai, who was prepared to rule as Suleiman's vassal, rather than Ferdinand as a candidate for the throne. The comparative religious toleration practised by the conquerors also strengthened the Ottoman position, at least in the short term; for the rapid spread of Protestantism through Turkish-occupied Hungary during the remainder of the sixteenth century made it unlikely that those members of the nobility who were converted to the reformed religion would rise in support of a prospective Habsburg and Catholic reconquest.

Abandoning for the time being any hope of recovering the heartland of the lost Hungarian kingdom, Habsburg policy narrowed to a series of attempts to detach the outlying vassal province of Transylvania from the Ottoman system. Intrigues and small-scale hostilities began in 1551 and continued until 1562, when Ferdinand was obliged to confirm the treaty of 1547. After Ferdinand's death in 1564 his successor, Maximilian II, resumed the offensive against Transylvania. It was to strengthen the Ottoman position in this region that Suleiman marched into Hungary on his last campaign of 1566. Although this expedition was abandoned on the death of the Sultan, it ensured continuation of the uneasy *status quo*.

The same pattern of violence and intrigue in Transylvania persisted throughout the later sixteenth and the seventeenth centuries, finding ultimate expression in the long and inconclusive war between Austria and the Turks from 1593 to 1606. For practical purposes, however, an uneasy stalemate in the Balkans had been reached in the 1540s and was confirmed by the events of the 1550s and 1560s. The Habsburg cause was weakened by family quarrels and the rumblings of the religious and political conflicts which were to erupt in the Thirty Years War. The Ottoman empire was at the same time affected by internal stresses and by military liabilities in the east: an expedition to Astrakhan in 1569–70, and hostilities against Persia from 1577 to 1590. The great sixteenth-century Turkish offensive in the Balkans had degenerated into a series of obscure, formless and indecisive frontier wars.

THE MEDITERRANEAN

During the sixteenth century naval operations played for the first time a major role in Ottoman attack and European defence. The capture of Constantinople, with its arsenal and access to the timber resources of Greece and the Black Sea, stimulated Turkish development as a sea power. The conquest of Syria and Egypt enormously lengthened the coastline of the Ottoman empire, adding large ports and populations with maritime traditions and experience to the

58 Andrea Doria, ruler of Genoa and Grand-Admiral of Spain from 1528 to 1560

sultan's dominion. Once established in Egypt, the Ottomans were also able to enter into close relations with their co-religionists in the chain of pirate states along the North African coast from Tripoli to Morocco, who contributed naval technicians and a succession of brilliant corsair admirals.

The Christian Mediterranean witnessed a similar expansion of sea power during the struggle for dominion of Italy between France and Spain in the late fifteenth and early sixteenth centuries. The *condottieri*, the professional soldiers, took to the water, covering the passage of armies through coastal areas and undertaking the movement of bullion, supplies and intelligence which were the nerves and sinews of French and Spanish imperialism. The career of the Genoese, Andrea Doria, illustrates the trend. Initially a mercenary soldier, he did not turn his interests to the sea until 1512, when he

59 The victory of the Holy Alliance of Spain, Venice and the Papacy at Lepanto in the Gulf of Corinth (1571) was widely celebrated in contemporary European literature and art.

was aged 46. Thereafter, as admiral of France, the Papacy and finally of Spain, he presided over a rapid extension of maritime conflict. He began his career with a private force of two galleys, which had increased to a squadron of twelve when he deserted from France to Spain in 1528. In 1537 he led a fleet of forty-five Spanish, eighty Venetian and twenty-six Papal galleys against the Turk.

This was the last great set-piece naval battle between Turks and Europeans in the sixteenth-century Mediterranean

The scale of naval operations continued to mount through the middle years of the century. At Lepanto in 1571 the Ottoman fleet comprised 230 and the Christian fleet 208 vessels. In the course of the engagement eighty Turkish galleys were sunk and 130 captured. Yet 'the infidel has only singed my beard; it will grow again', commented the Sultan; and Turkish losses were rapidly made good.

The construction, manning and provisioning of galleys on this scale laid heavy burdens on the technology and finances of the contending powers. One explanation of the diminishing intensity of Mediterranean naval war after the 1570s is that a point had been reached by both sides when the results obtainable were no longer commensurate with the expenditure of such immense resources.

The capture of Rhodes in 1522, following a year after that of Belgrade, announced Suleiman's intention of pursuing an offensive on two fronts and in two elements. A few European commercial outposts, notably Venetian Cyprus and Genoese Chios, were tolerated in the eastern Mediterranean, but the withdrawal of the Knights of St John from Rhodes to a new citadel on Malta marked the passing of crusading initiative in the Mediterranean from Christendom to Islam.

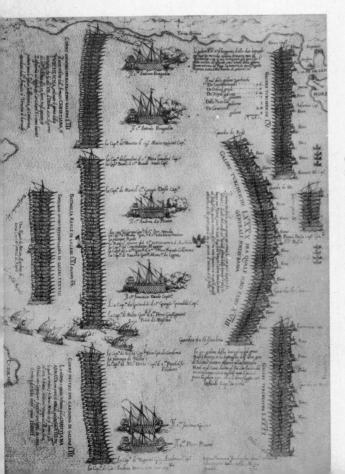

60 Plan showing disposition of fleets at the battle of Lepanto, 1571. The vanguard of the Ottoman fleet, under Ali Pasha, on the right, is drawn up in crescent formation. Six Venetian galleons, filled with soldiers, form the spearhead of the Christian fleet. The central squadron was commanded by Don John of Austria, that on his left by the Venetian admiral Barbarigo, that on his right by the Genoese Gian-Andrea Doria, and the rearguard by the Spaniard Santa Cruz

61 The appointment of the Algerian corsair, Khaireddin Barbarossa, as Pasha and Grand-Admiral of the Turkish fleet (1534) confirmed the alliance of the Ottoman empire with the North African pirate kingdoms

For a short while it seemed as if the advantage at sea might yet lie with European powers. In 1532 Andrea Doria commanded a Spanish expedition which stormed the Turkish outpost of Coron in the Morea. Two years later these hopes were extinguished; Khaireddin Barbarossa, 'king' of Algiers, the greatest of the corsair admirals, removed with his captains to Constantinople and placed himself at the disposition of the Sultan. Until his death in 1546 he led the 'war at sea' faction at Suleiman's court, imparting a decisive new naval emphasis to Ottoman policies.

In his new role as Ottoman admiral, Barbarossa began in spectacular fashion, capturing Tunis from a native ruler subservient to Spain. A laborious seaborne operation, led in person by Charles V, restored Spanish control over Tunis in 1535, but Barbarossa countered with savage raids against the coasts of Spain and the Balearics before the year was out.

The Ottomans struck again in 1537, attacking coastal towns in southern Italy and besieging the Venetian colony of Corfu from bases in the Adriatic. A hastily patched together alliance between Spain, Venice and the Papacy produced during the following year a large Christian fleet under Andrea Doria's command which continued operations in the same waters. Doria contacted Barbarossa's galleys off Prevesa, at the mouth of the Gulf of Arta. Ignoring the demands of his subordinates, especially the Venetian captains, whose

62 The recapture of Tunis by the Emperor Charles V in 1535 (right) brought little relief for Spain's Mediterranean dependencies from corsair depredations, and Tunis was recaptured by the Turks in 1574

natural first concern was to clear the Adriatic of enemy forces. Doria refused to commit himself to a decisive battle, engaging only in elaborate manœuvres and skirmishing in which his fleet was roughly handled. He was widely criticized for missing a rare opportunity of attacking a relatively small Turkish fleet, for contributing to the legend of Moslem invincibility which persisted until the battle of Lepanto, and for obliging the republic of Venice, which was unable to endure the strain of a long war, to sue for a peace which stripped her of valuable territories in the Morea and the Aegean archipelago. The chief consideration in his favour is that his strategic purpose was defensive, to shield Italy from attack or invasion, and, being uncertain of the reserve strength of the enemy, he was right to conserve his resources. One may also suspect that, as a Genoese, he was by no means averse to sacrificing the interests of Venice to those of the western Mediterranean powers.

Algiers remained the principal Moslem raiding base against Spain and Italy. Taking advantage of the military preoccupations

of Suleiman in Hungary, the Emperor Charles V launched and led in 1541 an expedition intended to seize the city and root out piracy. Storms disorganized the attack, dispersed the shipping and brought ruin on the enterprise. During the years which followed, the Ottomans threatened to break entirely free of the Spanish strategy of containment. In 1543, after the conclusion of a Franco-Turkish alliance, Barbarossa sacked Reggio and Nice and attacked the coasts of Catalonia. He wintered in Toulon, issuing in the spring of 1544 to raid the ports of Tuscany and the *Napoletano*. His death in 1546 brought no respite to Mediterranean Europe. Dragut, his ablest protégé, continued to attack Christendom from his North African strongholds. He seized Tripoli in 1551 and, until his death in Malta in 1565, terrorized Italy, Elba, Corsica, Catalonia and the Balearics. An expedition launched to drive him from Tripoli ended only in the defeat of a Spanish fleet and army at the island of Djerba in 1560. He was back in action immediately, blockading Naples during the summer of 1561.

These brilliant Turkish successes should not obscure the fact that the outlines of a strategic standstill in the Mediterranean, similar in many respects to that achieved on land in the Balkans, were already becoming apparent. For all the dash and vigour of their naval raids, the Moslems never succeeded in dislocating the structure of Spanish imperialism in the Mediterranean; captured none of the key islands, Sicily, Malta or Corsica; could never seriously contemplate an invasion of Italy.

The Spanish war effort in the Mediterranean improved when the throne passed in 1556 to Philip II, who did not inherit his father's heavy responsibilities in Germany and was freed by the Treaty of Cateau-Cambrésis (1559) from the dynastic struggle against France. More methodical if more narrow-minded than his father, Philip initiated in 1560 an ambitious programme of naval construction in the shipyards of Italy and Catalonia. A subsidy was received from the Papacy and in 1562 the Cortes of Castile was convened in extraordinary session to provide further financial backing.

63 The siege of Malta, 1565. The defeat of the Moslem invaders revealed the inability of the Ottomans and their North African allies to destroy Spanish naval power and achieve strategic domination of the western Mediterranean

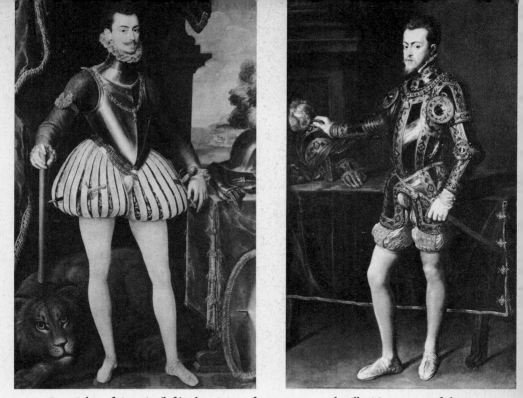

64, 65 Don John of Austria (left), the victor of Lepanto, was the illegitimate son of the Emperor Charles V and half-brother to Philip II (right), king of Spain from 1556 to 1598

The first fruit of this reorganization was the defeat of an Algerian attack on Oran in 1563, but its real test came with the Turkish siege of Malta in 1565. The island was overrun, but the defenders managed to cling to a few fortresses until a relieving expedition, mounted in Naples and Sicily, arrived to drive out the invaders.

Understanding of the final phase of the sixteenth-century Turkish seaborne offensive against Europe has traditionally been clouded by the insistence of western historians that its major episode, the Christian victory at Lepanto in 1571, marked a decisive shift in the balance of Mediterranean sea power. It did nothing of the sort. Hostilities opened with the Turkish seizure of Cyprus from Venice in 1570. The following year a combined Christian fleet under Don John of Austria met and defeated a much larger Turkish force at Lepanto near the mouth of the Gulf of Corinth. This was a notable

97

and well-organized victory; but the Turks retained Cyprus, rapidly rebuilt their navy, forced the withdrawal of Venice from the Christian alliance in 1573 and conquered Tunis in 1574. The real significance of the battle was that it ended an era of large and ambitious Mediterranean naval operations. The costs of such operations had become prohibitive. Both Spain and the Ottoman empire were increasingly preoccupied by events outside the Mediterranean. Peace negotiations were opened in 1577 and a formal truce was concluded in 1581, which was renewed in 1584 and again in 1587.

Spain was far from being freed entirely from Moslem pressure. The grumbling morisco problem at home and the depredations of North African corsairs persisted well into the seventeenth century. But after the 1570s, like the Balkan theatre and at about the same point in time, the Mediterranean fell temporarily into the background of history.

THE OTTOMAN OFFENSIVE: BALANCE OF SUCCESS AND FAILURE

The prolonged sea and land warfare recorded above follows a clear general pattern of outstanding initial success by Ottoman arms, degenerating into a situation in which, for the time being, neither side was capable of obtaining a decisive advantage. Until the resumption of the Ottoman offensive against Europe in the mid-seventeenth century, piracy and border brigandage flourished in areas which had become accustomed to the operations of great fleets and armies. What explains this trend of events?

The initial success of the Turks resulted from the coincidence of Ottoman efficiency with European disunity. By the sixteenth century the Turks had added to the fighting skills of a nomad people a sophistication of military organization unmatched in Europe until the seventeenth century. We may cite the example of Suleiman's Hungarian campaign in 1543, with its utilization of camel trains and river shipping, the skilful blending of specialist corps of engineers and artillery with regular and irregular infantry and cavalry units, entrustment of tactical command to local *begs* familiar with the ground – the entire operation conducted at an immense distance from the home bases of Adrianople and Constantinople. At the centre of this system stood the household infantry, the *élite* corps of janissaries, recruited from the child tribute of the Balkans, their obedience ensured by their slave status and their dedication to the profession of arms guaranteed by the incentive of plunder and by the prohibition – until the late sixteenth century – of both marriage and the practice of civilian trades.

This formidable military organization was more efficiently directed than any in contemporary Europe. The slave system of entry to the military-administrative profession opened careers to talent and permitted the rapid ascent of successful leaders to supreme command. The absence of any distinction between military and administrative authority and the concentration of supreme power in the person of the sultan tended to minimize those disputes and recriminations which disfigured European military practice. Ottoman rulers of the sixteenth century were seldom oppressed by such labours as those undertaken by Philip II in holding together the quarrelsome and mistrustful alliance of Spain, Venice and the Papacy from 1570 to 1573.

Behind the Ottoman military machine lay enormous resources of human energy. Perpetual superiority in manpower was a large factor in Turkish success. The absolute character of the sultan's authority, the weakness of family ties in Ottoman society and the opportunities offered during the sixteenth century for profit from the plunder of weak Christian neighbours in the Balkans and the Mediterranean guaranteed the mobilization of armies whose endurance and enthusiasm made them qualitatively as well as quantitatively superior to their European opponents. These advantages were reinforced by the inefficiencies and divisions of Christendom. The ponderous and undisciplined heavy cavalry which was still, in the sixteenth and early seventeenth centuries, the mainstay of eastern European armies was perpetually in difficulties against the light and mobile mounted forces of the Turks. As the English traveller, Moryson, observed:

the advantage of the Turkes horse swift to pursue or save themselves over the horse of Germany, howsoever able to endure assault, yet uppon any disaster unfitt to escape by flight and other advantages of warre on the Turkes part many and easy to be named, have made the Germans unable to withstand the great power of the Turkes.

The whole concept of military operations against the Turks was also fatally entangled with memories and traditions of chivalry and the crusades. Refusing to learn from the experience of the disastrous crusade of Nicopolis in 1396 and the abortive crusade of Pope Pius II in 1464, European rulers still nourished plans for vast counteroffensives like the *espedizione universale di tutta Cristianità contro a Selim principe dei Turchi*' projected by Pope Leo X in 1518. Even a relatively hardheaded secular statesman like Charles V was prone to such enthusiasms. Only long and bitter experience of unsuccessful warfare against the Ottomans produced, in the course of the sixteenth century, a more realistic and defensive strategy, exemplified by the fortification system created by Ferdinand I in Habsburg Hungary. Long-standing political divisions frustrated most European attempts to concert action against the Ottoman enemy. After the fall of Constantinople, the humanist, Aeneas Sylvius, the future Pope Pius II, deplored the disunity of Christendom:

> It is a body without a head, a republic without laws or magistrates . . . every state has a separate prince, and every prince has a separate interest . . . Who will make the English love the French? Who will unite the Genoese and the Aragonese? Who will reconcile the Germans with the Hungarians and Bohemians? . . . If you lead a small army against the Turks you will easily be overcome; if a large one, it will soon fall into confusion.

The sixteenth century saw no improvement in this situation, as was shown by the faction fights in Hungary in 1526 and the opposition of the German princes to the Emperor Charles V.

Political divisions merged into social conflicts. The social fragility which had delivered the medieval Serbian empire to Ottoman conquest was also characteristic of sixteenth-century Hungary.

66 Pius II (Aeneas Sylvius Piccolomini), who devoted his pontificate (1458–64) to abortive preparations for a crusade to recapture Constantinople, is here depicted exhorting an assembly at Mantua

Significantly, the Hungarian peasant revolt of 1514 evolved from a projected crusade against the Turks; and on the eve of Mohacs the papal nuncio, reporting on the condition of the kingdom, wrote: 'Among the Estates reign hate and need. And the subjects would, if the Sultan promises them freedom, raise an even more gruesome revolt against the nobles.' Peasant populations, not only in Danubian Europe but also in the Mediterranean colonies of the Italian maritime republics, frequently looked to the Turks as liberators. Neither in Genoese Chios in 1566 nor in Venetian Cyprus in 1570 did the Orthodox peasantry rally, in face of Turkish invasion, to the support of an Italian ruling class which was alien in language and religion, and brutally efficient in its methods of exploitation.

101

As the last examples suggest, social and political differences were reinforced by divergent sectarian tendencies. The Ottoman offensive of the sixteenth century burst upon a Europe convulsed by the great crisis of the Reformation. A succession of popes seized the opportunity of preaching the defence of Christendom as a means of restoring Christian unity, but the Reformation soon became too entangled in politics for this aim to succeed. The Balkans had long been a breeding ground of heresy, nurturing creeds like that of the Bogomils in medieval Bosnia, Serbia and Macedonia, whose differences with Roman Catholic authorities contributed to the ease of fifteenth century Ottoman conquests in these regions. In the sixteenth century Turkish military victories intensified the religious divisions of eastern Europeans. Hungarian Catholicism was paralyzed by the catastrophe of Mohacs, where seven of the sixteen bishops of the kingdom died on the battlefield. Profiting from this situation and tolerated by the Turks as fellow iconoclasts, Protestant missionaries made rapid headway in the conquered areas. The spread of Protestantism not only divided Europeans at a time of maximum Turkish pressure, but also reduced the possibility of substantial Christian reconquest of lost territories. Transylvania, for example, was a hot-bed of competing versions of Christianity, Catholicism, Lutheranism, Calvinism and Unitarianism all becoming deeply entrenched. The Protestant gentry viewed with small enthusiasm and occasional active opposition the prospect of being 'liberated' from vassalage to the sultan by Catholic Austria during the period of the Counter-Reformation.

Despite initial Ottoman triumphs produced by this combination of circumstances, the long wars of the sixteenth century arrived eventually at a situation of strategic deadlock. On land, this situation was foreshadowed by the Turkish failure to follow their victory at Mohacs in 1526 by the capture of Vienna in 1529. Even after his success in bringing central Hungary under direct Ottoman control during the 1540s, Suleiman was unable to achieve any further major victories or advances; and his last campaign in 1566 left the balance of power along the Balkan frontier virtually unaltered. The explanation lay in the limitations of even the most developed technical resources of the period in face of geographical difficulties and stiffening opposition.

The huge size of Turkish armies posed heavy commissariat problems. Their large cavalry component prohibited winter campaigns because of inadequate supplies of fodder and the unsuitability of winter ground conditions for mounted operations. The Turks were therefore restricted to summer campaigns, usually extending from mid-April to late October. Hungary, which was normally a 90–100 days' march from Constantinople, represented the exhaustion point of Ottoman military capacity.

It might have been otherwise had the European societies with which the Turks were in contact after Mohacs been as fragile and divided as those previously encountered in the Balkans, permitting rapid conquest and easy exploitation. But in central Europe firmly structured societies now barred the path of further Ottoman advance. The Turks found it increasingly difficult to make headway against a steepening cultural gradient whose impassable crown was the well-developed and articulated society solidified by common religious loyalties and deeply-rooted political institutions which occupied the Marchfeld plain around Vienna. Europeans here displayed much greater will and capacity to resist than the victims of the Ottomans in preceding centuries. This resistance found expression in the assumption of the crown of Hungary by Ferdinand of Austria in 1526. During the 1530s Ferdinand established in Habsburg Hungary a primitive, but deep and effective fortification system, and subsidized the 'grenzers' and uskoks, the violent and predatory frontier populations of Slavonia and Croatia, to operate as border raiders and pirates against the Turks. Such measures slowed and finally stopped the advance of Ottoman armies which were now campaigning at the limit of their operational capacity.

In the Mediterranean a parallel stalemate, concluding the period of spectacular Ottoman success which began in the 1520s, took shape during the 1560s and 1570s and was confirmed by the peace negotiations of 1577 and the truce of 1581. This left the Turks supreme in the eastern Mediterranean and firmly in possession of the principal North African bases of Algiers, Tripoli and Tunis. European control

67, 68 These ferociously armed 'grenzers', or frontiersmen, were provided with tenures along the Habsburg frontier with Turkish Hungary in return for military service. Grenzer regiments continued to play an important role in the Austrian military system until their amalgamation into the regular army in 1747. Note the similarity of the costume and accoutrements of the mounted grenzer to those of the *sipahi* in illustration 34

of the western Mediterranean was bought at the price of resolute protection of Italy, Sicily and Malta and the adoption of an alert defensive posture against corsair activities. But with the Spanish monarchy able and willing to pay this price, the Turks proved incapable of extending their dominion further westwards.

This maritime deadlock sprang from causes similar to those which were in operation on land in the Balkans. Professor Braudel has stressed the enormous dimensions of the sixteenth-century Mediterranean world when measured against the relatively feeble development of marine technology. The average journey by sea from Constantinople to Alexandria took 15 days, that from Constantinople to Venice took 34. Complete domination of Mediterranean waters was well beyond the technical and administrative resources of any one of the surrounding societies.

Most important, no serious movement of shipping, as on land no serious movement of armies, was possible during the winter months. Winter annually severed effective contact between Constantinople and remote raiding bases like Algiers. Corsair expeditions could be extremely damaging and disruptive, as the careers of Barbarossa and Dragut demonstrate, but the sailing season was too short and the problems of communication and supply were too complicated to permit conquest of distant strategic centres. As on land in eastern Europe the situation might have been different had European resistance been particularly weak and disorganized; but after Andrea Doria became the admiral of Spain in 1528, the Ottomans encountered competent opposition, which stiffened considerably as a result of the naval reforms of Philip II and the convoy system brought into operation on the Barcelona-Genoa axis during the 1570s and 1580s.

The Turkish failure to take Malta confirmed this situation. The short season available (the Turkish squadrons left Constantinople in April and the siege was raised in September), the strength of the island's fortifications and the provision of external assistance to the defenders from Spanish forward bases in Sicily made Malta the Vienna of the Mediterranean.

69 Turkish galleys were less reliable than their European counterparts, but could be constructed in large numbers and at great speed in the shipyards of the Ottoman empire and Algiers. The oarsmen were usually captive slaves or sailors enlisted from the ports of the Adriatic and Aegean

Noisent ARe Inuen: Iohan Kele Pfaler Schulpsit.

70 An allegorical representation of the might of the Ottoman empire. Posed against the background of the Golden Horn, the Turk stands supreme before the lowered standards of Europe, Africa and Asia. Symbols of ecclesiastical and secular authority in the Christian world are scattered about his feet

IV THE OTTOMAN IMPACT

In traditional accounts of early modern European history, the Ottomans generally figured as ominous noises-off, and were only ushered directly on stage for the purpose of being 'decisively' defeated at Lepanto. In one important respect, however, their presence was held to have contributed significantly to European development. By constricting the flow of oriental trade – particularly the essential traffic in spices – to Europe through the ports of the Levant, they were supposed to have been responsible for the European break-out to the west, which began in the fifteenth century with the exploration of the Atlantic coast of Africa and culminated in the Portuguese thrust to India and the Far Eastern spice islands and in the Spanish colonization of the New World.

On chronological grounds alone this was never a convincing interpretation. From Portugal, Henry the Navigator's captains were purposefully engaged on the circumnavigation of Africa before the Turks had even captured Constantinople. Vasco da Gama reached the Malabar coast of India and Afonso de Albuquerque threw a network of fortified trading stations across the Far East and the Indian Ocean before Selim I conquered the *entrepôts* of Syria and Egypt.

So far from Portuguese initiatives being a result of Ottoman interference with the spice trade, the reverse, if anything, is nearer the truth. From 1505 until the death of King Manuel I in 1521 the Portuguese, working from their newly-acquired bases in East Africa and Asia, followed a deliberate – and in the short run highly successful – policy of eliminating all Moslem interests from the commerce in spices. An exultant Portuguese contemporary wrote: 'Mohammed is cornered and cannot go further and flees as much as he can . . . and the truth is that Mohammed will be destroyed and destroyed he cannot help but be.'

Ottoman campaigns and commercial policy after 1515 may be interpreted as an energetic response to this crisis. The invasion of Syria and Egypt in 1516–17 established Turkish control over Cairo, Alexandria and Beirut, the principal spice ports of the Levant. The seizure of Rhodes in 1522 was essential to the security of the sea-lanes between these centres and Constantinople. These conquests provide the background to the efforts made by the Ottoman government in 1520 and again in 1530 to exclude the traditional monopolists and profiteers of the spice trade, the merchants of Syria, Egypt and Venice, by concentrating the spice market in Constantinople under official supervision, and exporting to Europe along the Danube rather than by sea to Italy. Suleiman's Balkan campaigns of the 1520s and early 1530s then fall logically into place as attempts to establish control over the entire length of the Danube trade route into Germany. This is not the record of a government intent on strangling the spice trade. The thesis that Ottoman expansion compelled Iberian exploration cannot therefore be sustained.

In a profounder sense, however, the two episodes may have been connected. Medieval Europe was a constricted society, subject to perpetual heavy pressure from the east. The crusades brought no permanent relief from this Moslem blockade. Yet by the close of the fifteenth century, European economic activity was becoming increasingly, if irregularly, intense. Population was rising; agricultural investment grew notably in volume; technological innovation improved productivity in the textile and extractive industries. The economic pre-conditions of an 'expansion of Europe' were already present. Simultaneously the Ottomans established their empire in the Balkans, the Black Sea areas and the Levant. Moslem dominion over these regions was extended and solidified beyond any hope of overthrow. Expansive forces in the European economy were therefore obliged to find their outlet at an initially unpromising, but eventually immensely rewarding point of less formidable resistance, in the far west. The Turks did not propel Europeans in this direction; they simply sealed off the alternative exits.

Analysis of the Ottoman impact on Renaissance and Reformation Europe can profitably concentrate on less speculative themes and more demonstrable consequences than the above. The difficulty, as always in assessing the effect of an external influence on the evolution of a society or group of societies, is that of disentangling the operations of this factor from those of the myriad other forces which interacted with it and each other to make up the pattern of events. This book makes no attempt to unravel such complicated chains of causation. Certain areas upon which the Ottoman impact was obvious and direct are singled out for separate and extremely selective discussion. Developments in each area were a consequence of the same basic crisis: the collapse of the frontier between Christianity and Islam under Ottoman pressure.

A frontier, in this context, is not a line on a map – a boundary – but the transitional zone between different cultures or social structures. In periods of stability and equilibrium the frontier tends to be a relatively neglected but frequently turbulent strip of territory whose local restlessness has an ultimate tranquillizing effect by preventing abrasive confrontations between the societies which it holds apart. When, on the other hand, such societies fall into profound conflict, each tends to become, as it were, a function of its frontier. For the aggressive, expansive society the frontier now represents the point of maximum outward thrust or pressure, whether of population or military forces; the task of extending the frontier attracts and mobilizes the totality of social energies. For the society which is being constricted and attacked the frontier is transformed from an indifferently regarded limitrophic area into a 'Great Wall', the defence of which becomes the highest priority among those who rely upon its protection.

Created by one of many historic waves of nomad conquest from central Asia, the Ottoman empire was sustained by the ceaseless acquisition and digestion of plunder. Expansion of the frontier was its law of life. Europe, although constricted, was not intolerably hard-pressed by Ottoman activities so long as the ramparts formed by the Serbian and Byzantine empires and the Hungarian kingdom remained intact and the Turks had not yet established themselves as a Mediterranean sea power. Mounting Ottoman pressure from the fourteenth century onwards culminated in the sixteenth century in a spectacular breakthrough. With Suleiman's armies at the gates of Vienna and his navies terrorizing the central and western Mediterranean, the traditional frontier had collapsed. The Turks no longer represented a serious nuisance but a deadly danger.

Naturally, the remote and sheltered northern and western sectors of European society remained relatively undisturbed; but key areas of European civilization, the German lands and the Italian peninsula, were now exposed to attack. Men of letters, much given to classical allusion, gloomily recalled the destruction of the Roman frontiers by barbarian invaders. Preachers and pamphleteers held the Turks to be the irresistible instruments of divine displeasure with an errant and degenerate Christian society.

Our task is to take some soundings of European experience and reaction under the physical and psychological shock of this Turkish assault.

THE ZONE OF OTTOMAN CONQUEST: BALKAN AND DANUBIAN EUROPE

The condition of those European peoples who were conquered or cut off by Ottoman advance in the fifteenth and sixteenth centuries varied considerably according to local circumstance. A few inaccessible or outlying areas were never subjected to direct Ottoman rule or colonization, being allowed a certain autonomy on payment of tribute or performance of specific services. Notable among these was the republic of Ragusa (Dubrovnik). A typical medium-sized Italian merchant commune situated on the Adriatic fringe of the Balkan peninsula, Ragusa subsisted during the late Middle Ages by organizing the exchange of European manufactured goods for grain, hides, slaves and raw metals from the interior. The jealous competition of Venice and the chronic political instability of the Balkan hinterland perpetually endangered this enterprise.

The Ottoman conquest of Bosnia (1463) and Herzegovina (1482) hemmed the republic into a tiny territorial confine and reduced it to absolute dependence on the goodwill of the sultan. Payment of substantial tribute – fixed during the late fifteenth century at 12,500 ducats per annum, a sum which remained constant over centuries –

bought immunity from actual invasion. Ragusans were in fact too useful to the Turks for conquest to be worth while. Ragusan merchant communities in Niš, Novibazar and Skopje animated the whole economy of the Balkans, undertaking essential economic activities in which the Turks were generally incompetent or uninterested. They monopolized the salt trade of the region; served the sultan and his Balkan *begs* as customs officials and tax collectors; imported European textiles; and exported Albanian zinc and Bosnian lead to Italy. Secular and ecclesiastical ornaments fashioned by Ragusan craftsmen from the gold and silver of Bosnian and Serbian mines found ready markets in Rome, Venice and Constantinople.

The conquests of Suleiman and the naval wars of the sixteenth century conferred on the republic the benefits of a brief and precarious golden age. As their Black Sea colonies crumbled and disappeared under Turkish pressure, the Genoese turned from freighting and ship-building to contracting and finance. Venetian shipping also disintegrated under corsair attacks and the strain of prolonged naval operations. Ragusans filled the gap which these developments opened in the Mediterranean carrying trade. While Venetian commerce was paralyzed during the war of Cyprus (1570–3), sixty 'great ships' of Ragusa were plying between Constantinople, Alexandria, Tripoli, Beirut and Salonika. There were 250 registered masters and 5,000 seamen in the port during the early 1580s, and 200 merchant vessels in operation.

71 A merchant of Ragusa. The capacious Ragusan 'carracks' obtained a large share of the eastern Mediterranean carrying trade during the sixteenth century, and the Ragusans were privileged tradesmen and entrepreneurs in all the European provinces of the Ottoman empire

Ragusa also provided a necessary point of contact and communication between Europe and the Ottoman empire. The city was the Adriatic starting point of the caravan route which conducted merchants and diplomatists through Niš, Sofia and Philippopolis to Constantinople. Ragusan spies and secret agents were active in the underworld of European politics. During the 1530s, while one Ragusan merchant, Serafin Gučetić, was initiating the negotiations which led to the Franco-Turkish agreement of 1536, another, Marin Zamanja, was making regular reports on Ottoman affairs to the Emperor Charles V.

The prosperity which these activities bestowed on the merchant and manufacturing oligarchy enabled them to perpetuate their power by freezing the social relationships of the republic in a traditional mould. At a time when the towns of mainland Italy were racked by class conflicts and being absorbed into the structure of territorial states, Ragusa remained a fossilized medieval commune whose economic and political activities were controlled by a college of socially exclusive and highly regulated gilds.

The mountaineers of Montenegro, like the townsmen of Ragusa, were isolated but not engulfed by the tides of Ottoman conquest. The Turks invaded and occupied the region in 1496, but the remoteness and difficulty of the terrain soon caused them to abandon a policy of colonization in favour of loose and nominal suzerainty. A *voivod*, elected from the local magnates, was responsible for the collection and delivery of a general tax; but the real currency with which Montenegro purchased freedom from interference was military service by the tribesmen of the region in the armies of the sultan. The opportunities for plunder which became available under this arrangement guaranteed, at least during the sixteenth century, the enthusiastic participation of Montenegrin clan chieftains in Ottoman military operations.

It is difficult to arrive at an accurate general assessment of post-conquest conditions in the 'occupied' plains and cultivated lands south of the Danube. There is much evidence that during the fifteenth and sixteenth centuries the peasant populations of the Balkans and central Hungary often welcomed and frequently assisted the

Ottoman advance. The explanation lies in the more primitive and less exacting character of Turkish feudalism in comparison with its European counterpart. The methods and attitudes of the hereditary gentry and nobility of Serbia, Bosnia and Croatia in the fifteenth century and of Hungary in the sixteenth were distinguished from those current in central and western Europe only by a greater degree of brutality. Ottoman feudalism, in contrast, was based on the social institution of the *timar*, an uninheritable fief made over to the *sipahi*, the mounted warrior, in return for his services in war. From the point of view of the peasants the advantages of this system were considerable. Their lord was usually absent on camapign for the entire summer, and more interested in booty acquired there than in exactions from his serfs and tenants as a source of income. Customary dues were rendered more often in labour and services than in money or goods. The uninheritable character of the *timar*, and the weakness of family ties in Turkish society made the Ottoman *sipahi* far less interested than his Christian counterpart in making increased provision for his descendants by such practices as rack-renting.

There was therefore less opportunity and incentive for landlords to practice extreme exploitation than in European feudalism. They were further inhibited, at least until the seventeenth century, by the absence of manorial courts on the western model. Judicial administration was monopolized by a watchful and omnipotent central government whose agents at all levels were usually slaves of Balkan origin who retained a residual loyalty to and compassion for the village societies from which they sprang.

It would be wrong, however, to suppose that benevolence was a guiding principle of Ottoman colonial policy. Certainly the child tribute exacted from the remote regions of the western Balkans, which maintained the manpower of the imperial household and the janissary corps from the fifteenth century until its discontinuation in 1638, occasioned comparatively little resentment. This is understandable if we contrast the conditions and opportunities of life in the royal training establishments of Constantinople with the miseries and privations of Bosnian and Albanian village existence.

In more affluent areas, however, the Ottomans proved to be vigilant and demanding tax collectors. Christian subjects who did not perform important military or administrative duties paid, in addition to the universal land tax, a substantial poll tax, the *harač*. Nor did the arrival of the Turks always ease the burdens imposed by native landlords. In parts of Bosnia, Serbia, Macedonia and Hungary some local gentry survived the conquest, bribing Ottoman officials to confirm them in their privileges or re-establishing themselves in a new role as Turkish *sipahis*, so that the oppressive traditional rural regime persisted virtually intact.

Much suffering and privation was inflicted upon the Hungarian peasantry by the prolonged wars of the sixteenth century, when the no-man's-land of the central Hungarian plain was repeatedly despoiled by contending armies. In the county of Bereg, for example, nine of the eleven towns were pillaged and 4,200 of the 6,000 peasant holdings laid waste during the second half of the sixteenth century. In some areas the serfs were coerced into payment of double tribute – to a Turkish *sipahi* and to an hereditary Christian lord who would emerge from prudent obscurity once the Ottoman warrior had left for the summer campaign. Inevitably there was much depopulation and abandonment of open country. Some peasants fled to the security of towns and large villages. Others resorted to nomadic pastoralism, a less exposed and dangerous way of life than crop cultivation in a disturbed and lawless region. This tendency was reinforced, not only in Hungary but throughout Balkan and Danubian Europe, by the incidence of Ottoman taxation which fell much more heavily on arable land than on pasture. Landowners were thus encouraged to clear peasant cultivators from their estates to make way for sheep, goats and horses.

The revival of nomadic pastoralism provided a new lease of life for the Rumanian-speaking Vlachs, migratory herdsmen whose native principalities of Moldavia and Wallachia had fallen under Ottoman dominion during the fifteenth century. In these regions the boyars, or clan chieftains, responding to the demands of the expanding food market of sixteenth-century Constantinople, transformed themselves into a settled 'feudal' landlord class, depressing their once free followers into the status of servile cattle-raisers and cultivators. But outside their homeland Vlach communities continued to roam freely and widely. Their relations with the Turks were closer and more cordial than those of other Balkan peoples, being based on the mutual understanding between nomadic peoples. As the principal horse breeders and dealers of the Balkans they were invaluable to the commissariat of Ottoman armies. In return they obtained a monopoly of certain marginal occupations, serving as bodyguards to itinerant imperial officials and as guides and escorts to merchant caravans.

During the second half of the sixteenth century, the condition of the peasants of the conquered lands of south-eastern Europe underwent a marked and general decline. The military deadlock between Europe and Islam on the Danube sharply diminished Turkish prospects of plunder. *Sipahis* began to compensate themselves for the subsequent loss of income by increasing the severity of the economic demands which they made on their tenants. In many cases they successfully evaded the law and subverted the *timar* system by transforming their estates into inheritable fiefs. The consequent rapid evolution of a rooted hereditary aristocracy simultaneously exposed the peasants to harsher measures of economic exploitation and reduced the capacity of the central government to restrict the excesses of landlords. The outcome was a series of peasant risings of which the best documented, but by no means isolated, example was the running revolt round Mariovo and Prilep in 1564-5.

We must not exaggerate the significance of such symptoms. If the condition of the peasantry in the Turkish-occupied Balkan and Danubian lands deteriorated in the course of the sixteenth century, it probably remained – with the exception of central Hungary, which was exposed to particular afflictions – superior to that of the serfs in most Christian states of eastern and central Europe. The Mariovo revolt, for instance, was paralleled by a much larger peasant rising against the landlords of Habsburg Croatia and Slovenia in 1573. And – again excluding the region of war and plunder in Hungary – the increasingly effective incorporation of south-eastern Europe into the Ottoman system compensated for occasional troubles in the countryside by stimulating urban development – evident in the rise of important new commercial centres like Sarajevo and Novibazar – and producing a general increase in population from about 1550.

The Turks, then, though frequently neglectful and cruel, were seldom systematically tyrannical. Especially notable, when contrasted with the missionary passion and sectarian intolerance of contemporary Europe, was the very high degree of religious toleration accorded to their alien subjects. Islamization proceeded slowly in the Balkans, where the process of conversion seems to have been linked much more closely to considerations of private social or economic advantage – particularly the anticipation of freedom for the convert from certain forms of taxation or obligatory government service – than to any strenuous proselytizing policy followed by Ottoman administrators. On the other hand, the very absence of an energetic policy of conversion perpetuated a gulf in religious sensibility and practice between Christian subjects and Moslem rulers. This fundamental lack of sympathy and contact between the two groups, 'who met', according to one historian, 'only in vice', was to prove, in the long run, fatal to Turkish prospects of establishing their power permanently in south-eastern Europe.

Visions, which may still be current in popular imagination, of the

72, 73 When addressing a popular audience, Christian propagandists of the sixteenth century tended to project familiar images of evil on to the Moslems. Conventional woodcuts such as those on the right, depicting the Massacre of the Innocents and the cult of devil worship, were crudely and uncritically included as illustrations to literary diatribes against the Turks

116

Christian peoples of the Balkans languishing in total and hopeless subjection to bloodthirsty conquerors are the products either of the propaganda put out at the time by spokesmen for 'crusading' interests, notably the Habsburgs and the Papacy, or of a modern tendency to impose on the sixteenth century a picture of the situation derived from the very different conditions of the nineteenth, when the dying Ottoman empire was desperately seeking to stamp out the flames of Balkan nationalism. These are grotesque caricatures of the truth. Yet recent historians, rightly searching for a more balanced verdict, have perhaps allowed themselves to be over-impressed by the evidence that in many areas the Turks were welcomed as liberators rather than feared as aggressors. For, whatever the initial advantages from the point of view of the lower classes, the long-term experience of absorption into the Ottoman empire was a tragedy for south-eastern Europe. There was something sterile about Ottoman imperialism. The conquered European peoples were imprisoned for some centuries within a social and political system which lacked the capacity for sustained development; whose values were fundamentally uncritical and uncreative; and whose élites found it impossible to advance beyond an ideal of violent and voluptuous parasitism. This has proved, in the period since the disappearance of Turkey-in-Europe, a difficult and oppressive heritage.

Throughout the length and breadth of the European society against which Suleiman launched his attacks, ruling dynasties were engaged upon the erosion of the power and privileges of urban centres and local lords. In this enterprise the formula for success was always and everywhere the same: increases in taxation; expansion of bureaucracy; and the creation of professional standing armies.

Among the princely houses of Europe the Habsburgs were distinguished by neither heroism nor intelligence; but their tenacity was unequalled, their ambition unbounded and their luck phenomenal. As archdukes of Austria, the family meddled impartially in the politics of the Danube lands and in those of the Holy Roman Empire. They were particularly alarmed by the emergence and aggressive attitudes of the large Hungarian kingdom created by Matthias Corvinus during the fifteenth century, which betrayed as yet no hint of its eventual weakness. Skilful diplomatic activity turned the situation to the advantage of the Habsburgs by a treaty between Austria and Hungary in 1463, when it was agreed that Hungary should pass into Habsburg hands should Matthias die without heirs. The Habsburgs appeared to be opting for an 'eastern' emphasis in foreign policy. In fact, any such binding decision would have been alien to the nature of a dynasty whose only permanent commitment throughout its long career was to keep a clear eye to the main chance.

The Habsburgs were permanently interested in German politics after 1438, when the throne of the Holy Roman Empire became a family heirloom. And in 1477 the dynasty concluded its fateful marriage alliance with the ruling house of Burgundy. To be sure, the Habsburgs continued to finance a 'German' party among the Hungarian magnates and to play with their accustomed finesse the game of marriage alliances at the Hungarian court. But eastern Europe now assumed a secondary role in their political calculations, and they were disinclined to react violently when, on the death of Matthias Corvinus without issue in 1490, the crown of Hungary passed to the ruling family of Bohemia. Rich compensations were available elsewhere; and Habsburg ambitions appeared to be fully satisfied when the united houses of Austria and Burgundy were linked with those of Aragon and Castile by the marriage of Philip of Burgundy and Joanna the Mad in 1496. A chain of unforeseen and unforeseeable circumstances then conducted Charles – the eldest son of this marriage – to the thrones of the Netherlands in 1506, of Spain in 1516 and, as Charles V, to the Imperial dignity in 1519.

This sequence of events and the simultaneous explosion of Ottoman power in the eastern Mediterranean and on the Danube brought the Habsburgs into confrontation with the advancing Turks at a number of strategic points. As King of Spain, Charles V was obliged to undertake the task of organizing resistance to Moslem seaborne attacks upon his Italian dependencies and eventually upon the coastline of Spain itself. As Holy Roman Emperor he was acutely conscious of his role as guardian of Catholic Christendom against Islam.

Preoccupied by political difficulties in Spain and by the beginnings of the Lutheran revolt in Germany, Charles made over to his younger brother Ferdinand the lands of the Austrian inheritance, the duchies of Austria, Carinthia, Carniola, Styria and Tyrol, in 1521–2. Ferdinand was soon called upon to deal with a grave threat to the neglected but still essential interests of his dynasty in eastern Europe. The collapse of Hungary left the Austrian archduke occupying the front line of defence against the Turks. The death of King Lewis of Hungary, husband of Ferdinand's sister Mary and brother of his wife Anne, at Mohacs in 1526 made Ferdinand an automatic contender for the Hungarian crown. Suleiman's determined siege of Vienna in 1529 further revived and intensified the concern of the Habsburg dynasty with the future of Danubian Europe.

In Spain, in Spanish Italy and in eastern Europe the Habsburgs were forced to assume responsibility for the defence of long sectors of the European frontier zone. The subsequent bitter struggle between the dynasty and the Ottomans profoundly modified and influenced the historical development of these regions.

In Hungary Ferdinand encountered every difficulty. Two-thirds of the kingdom was dominated or occupied beyond hope of recovery by the Ottomans, and his claim to the remainder was fiercely contested by a rival candidate. But as head of the

Reichs-regiment, the administrative apparatus of the Holy Roman Empire, and as King of the Romans (and therefore prospective Emperor) after 1531, Ferdinand brought considerable resources to the tasks of consolidating Habsburg control over those north-western provinces of Hungary which remained outside the Ottoman system and of organizing frontier defences against further Turkish attacks.

So far as military operations were concerned, he was obliged to improvise. Charles V made it clear to his brother that the needs of Imperial Spain and the struggle against Protestantism in Germany prevented the concentration of great Habsburg armies in eastern Europe. Only once, in 1532, was the full might of Habsburg military power drawn up before Vienna. Apart from this isolated occasion, assistance was restricted to a sparse supply of Spanish, Italian and Walloon professional infantry. Yet these, though few in numbers, were effectively employed. Their discipline and techniques were a century in advance of the clumsy, old-fashioned and reckless military practices of the eastern European nobility. Distributed through a deep defensive system of small, crude forts which consisted of little more than primitive earthworks supported by wooden palisades, these experienced campaigners proved capable of delaying or bringing to a halt the progress of numerically immensely superior Turkish forces. By regularly compelling the Turks to expend the brief campaigning season in the reduction of a few insignificant fortified positions, they postponed for over a century a further Ottoman breakthrough comparable to that of 1526-9. Thus at Güns in 1532 the entire Turkish army under Suleiman's personal command was held up over a month by a garrison of less than 800 men.

For the defence of his southern border in Croatia and Slavonia, Ferdinand relied exclusively on local resources. From 1535 he entered into annual compacts with the 'grenzers', the untamed and heterogeneous frontier population whose resentment of any external authority might, in other circumstances, have constituted an intolerable embarrassment to the Habsburgs. By the terms of these agreements the 'grenzers' waged incessant private war against the Ottoman authorities on the other side of the frontier in return for financial subsidies and grants of conquered land.

The security of Habsburg Hungary from Turkish attack depended as much upon administrative measures as upon military dispositions; in particular, it was related to Ferdinand's success in ensuring local obedience to the will of the king and his bureaucrats in Vienna. He faced here a task of enormous difficulty and complexity. The Hungarian nobility – a numerous class ranging from great territorial magnates to obscure local gentry, faction-ridden in their internal politics, but remarkably united ('the one and indivisible nobility' in the stock phrase of their legal apologists) when their collective interests came under question – were deeply entrenched in both local and central government. The county assemblies, elected and manned by the nobles of the region, were provincial governments in permanent session, enacting legislation, executing policy and sitting in judgment upon their own acts. Needing the support of the nobility in the struggle against the Turks, Ferdinand dared make no inroads into this system of embedded aristocratic privilege and control. At the centre, however, where the great magnates dominated the Parliament and the Royal Council, he conducted a prolonged, resourceful and determined campaign aimed at incorporating Hungary into the wider framework and purposes of the Austrian state. The powers of the Royal Council were drastically reduced and even its effective successor, the *camerae administratio*, existed for little more than distribution of financial grants handed over to it by the central authorities in Vienna. The traditional office of palatine, whose incumbent, invariably a great nobleman, combined the functions of regent and official spokesman for aristocratic interests at court, was suspended temporarily in 1532 and permanently in 1562. The preparation of agendas for the Hungarian Parliament was taken out of its own hands and entrusted to the Imperial Privy Council (the *Geheimrat*) in Vienna. In 1547 Parliament was also induced to accept a statute which implicitly surrendered its right of electing the monarch and, in 1563, was persuaded to allow Ferdinand's successor to be crowned during his father's lifetime.

These real, if limited, royal and bureaucratic advances were supplemented by the success of the Habsburgs in gaining control of the administration and profits of the Hungarian tithe. This was the most ancient and general national tax-in-kind, originally intended for the upkeep of the Church and falling on all classes from the serfs to the nobility. During the late medieval centuries the collection of this levy passed into the hands of the lesser nobility, who diverted much of its yield from ecclesiastical purposes to their own profit. The nobility, thrown into temporary confusion and infirmity of purpose by the Ottoman triumphs of 1526-9 and recognizing the imperative need for substantial returns from taxation to be devoted to a system of national defence, largely surrendered the right of administration of the tithe to the crown. The yield was employed by Ferdinand and his successors in supplying the military forces who manned the frontier fortresses.

This development entailed curious social and political consequences. On the one hand, Habsburg administrative control over the Hungarian kingdom was strengthened and extended. On the other, resentment of the obligation to pay the tax – even when it was admitted to be necessary – on the part of Hungarian serfs and nobles promoted and solidified an unlikely alliance of these two groups against their Habsburg rulers. Thus, in the county of Heves in 1583 six serfs and a noble stood jointly accused of complicity in the evasion of tithes. The traditionally ferocious antagonism between social classes in Hungary was becoming mitigated in face of the impartial exactions of an Austrian overlord; and this process was reinforced by the experience of military cooperation between serfs and nobles against Turkish armies and raiding parties.

The complicated effect of sixteenth-century Turkish pressure on those European territories which lay beyond the Danubian frontier of the Ottoman empire may therefore be summarized as follows. The spectacularly successful early campaigns of Suleiman in the Balkans forced the Habsburgs to look again, after a period of comparative neglect, to the preservation of their dynastic interests on the Danube. They were obliged to devote considerable energy and ingenuity to the connected problems of enfolding the remnants of the old kingdom of Hungary into the Austrian administrative system and of organizing frontier defences capable of repelling further Ottoman attacks. Hungarian reluctance to submit unreservedly to the Habsburg embrace, together with the threatening Ottoman presence in the Balkans, ensured that Austrian rulers and bureaucrats would be engaged and entangled for a prolonged period by these problems. A new Habsburg state had been ushered into existence, with its capital at Vienna, involved in perpetual war with the Ottoman empire and saddled with an intractable Hungarian problem. To this extent the Austrian empire, one of the principal constituents of the European states system until its extinction in the twentieth century, was the unintentional creation of Suleiman the Magnificent. Of course the Austrian Habsburgs never became entirely reconciled to an exclusively Danubian destiny. During the seventeenth, eighteenth and nineteenth centuries they struggled to yoke all Germany to Vienna. Yet these projects ended in frustration and defeat; it was the permanent eastern European commitment, at first to defence against the Ottomans, then, as Turkish power diminished, to the *Drang nach Osten* which ultimately determined the character and evolution of the Austrian state.

THE SPANISH HABSBURGS AND THE OTTOMAN EMPIRE
On the Habsburg frontier in eastern Europe the overpowering weight and persistence of Ottoman pressure dictated the evolution and rhythm of events through most of the sixteenth century. The effects of Ottoman expansion on the Habsburg monarchy in Spain are more difficult to estimate. The rulers of sixteenth-century Spain were entangled in a network of problems, several of which were at least as burdensome and intractable as that presented by the Turks. There was the problem of tapping and transporting the vast mineral wealth of the American Indies; of quelling Lutheran and princely disobedience in Germany; of pursuing the dynastic rivalry with the Valois monarchy of France; of subduing revolt in the Netherlands; and finally of waging war against Elizabethan England. The inter-actions of each of these with the task of organizing resistance to Ottoman aggression were frequent and complicated.

Three factors urged Habsburg Spain towards conflict with the expansive Ottoman empire in the Mediterranean. Firstly, Charles V (1516–56) and Philip II (1556–98) inherited a Spanish state which

74, 75 Isabella, queen of Castile (d. 1504), and her husband, Ferdinand the Catholic, king of Aragon (d. 1516). Their marriage (1469) and conquest of the Moorish kingdom of Granada (1492) brought Spain for the first time under a united monarchy

had only recently been united by the marriage of Isabella of Castile and Ferdinand of Aragon in 1469. The interests and attitudes of the constituent kingdoms remained fundamentally separate. This was particularly true of foreign policy, where Aragon maintained traditions of imperialist expansion in the Balearic Islands, Sardinia, Malta, Naples and Sicily, with which Castile had never been associated. The union of the crowns, however, enabled Ferdinand to harness Castilian wealth and energy to Aragonese purposes and to prosecute successful warfare against France for dominion over southern Italy. He implanted a long-term strategy of Italian conquest as a guiding principle of Spanish foreign policy. This was inherited by Charles V and pursued so successfully that by the 1530s most of the Italian peninsula was in Spanish hands or under Spanish influence. During the same years the Ottoman and North African naval offensive against Christendom reached formidable proportions; Turkish navies and Algerian corsairs threatened to sweep the central

Mediterranean free of Christian commerce and shipping. This threat to Charles V's possessions and responsibilities in Italy left him no alternative but resistance.

Secondly, both Charles V and Philip II were products of a fiercely enthusiastic age of religious history. Each, for all his cynicism and capacity for compromise, treasured a concept of kingship in which the protection of true religion occupied an important place. It was as 'God's standard bearer' that Charles referred to himself when he embarked at Barcelona to lead the expedition against Tunis in 1535. The Spanish Habsburgs provided a mirror image of Moslem dedication to the *Jihad*; and when the Turks and their allies directed attacks upon the coastlines of the central and western Mediterranean, profound religious conviction as well as a lively sense of self-preservation stimulated the kings of Spain to assume the role of champions of Christendom.

In the third place, Spain, to a greater extent than any other European state, remained in the sixteenth century a crusading power. The Iberian kingdoms were created in the course of long wars against the Moors on territory won back from the infidel. In Spain crusading was an active profession as well as a hallowed tradition; the conquest of the Moorish kingdom of Granada had taken place as recently as 1492, and between 1502 and 1511 the military offensive was carried

76 Naval battle between Christians and Turks. Sixteenth- and seventeenth-century schools of Spanish painting frequently celebrated the persistence of Iberian crusading traditions

across the Mediterranean into Morocco. The sixteenth-century military and naval confrontation with the Ottoman empire was, from a Spanish viewpoint, the logical continuation of a struggle long ago undertaken and never since abandoned. And for Spaniards the inevitable ferocity of religious warfare was sharpened by the fact that the kingdom contained, as a result of the medieval Reconquest, a sizable population of Moors who had only very recently been subjected to the indignities of forced conversion to Christianity. The Spanish government, fearful that Ottoman expansion would encourage the Moslem minority at home to pass from resentment to open rebellion, hastened into action against the advancing Turks.

An outline account of the long wars in the Mediterranean between Habsburg Spain and the Ottoman empire has already been provided. This war effort imposed enormous strains upon Spanish society and the Spanish economy. Expeditions like those of Charles V against Algiers in 1541 and Gian-Andrea Doria against Djerba in 1560 threw away many thousands of soldiers and sailors and huge concentrations of expensive shipping to no significant purpose. To meet the costs of such exertions, taxation on the *pecheros*, the common classes of Spain, rose steeply, though the nobility remained largely exempt. Endemic poverty was inflicted upon the lower orders of society and permanent damage imposed on the growth prospects of the Spanish economy. The sixteenth-century influx of American treasure should have promoted and sustained impressive economic development. In fact, the weight of taxation deprived traders and manufacturers of potential customers and cruelly inhibited investment in new ventures. Theoretically, Spain was the wealthiest of European powers; but hers was a sterile prosperity, restricted to the unproductive classes.

The miseries of Spain were reflected in her Mediterranean dependencies. Many of these, situated in the front line of naval warfare against the Turks, were subjected to a tax burden equal to that borne by the mother country. In Sicily, Charles V's last two Viceroys, Ferrante Gonzaga and Juan de Vega, levied heavy local taxes for the construction of coastal defences, maintenance of a fleet of ten galleys and a *tercio* of Spanish infantry and the training of local militia to beat off Algerian pirate raids. Demands increased as Ottoman successes multiplied. Sicily was burdened with extraordinary taxes when a Turkish invasion was anticipated following the Christian disaster at Djerba in 1560. Next came demands for shipping and naval supplies when a fleet was assembling at Messina for the relief of Malta in 1565. The heaviest demands of all were made by Don John of Austria during the Lepanto campaign of 1571, when Sicily was the advance base for the operation of the Holy League. In 1573 the Sicilian President, Terranova, protested to Philip II that exactions had reached their absolute limit, and expressed fears for the stability of the Spanish regime on the island. By 1575 Sicily could contribute no more and Madrid was obliged to supplement the Sicilian budget.

A fairly precise measure of how directly these impositions were related to the requirements of Mediterranean warfare against the Turks is provided by a despatch from Sicily by President Colonna in 1581:

> . . . in the five years I have been here I have not asked this kingdom for a single *real* of extraordinary taxes . . . I have kept down ordinary and extraordinary expenses, have supplied all that His Majesty has asked of me, and have relieved this court of the greater part of its debts.

Evidently the situation had been transformed since 1575. The only possible explanation lies in the sharply reduced scale of naval operations in the years following Lepanto. Thus many – though by no means all – of Spain's economic difficulties were connected with Ottoman pressure and the high costs of resistance to it.

The same was true of numerous social problems, especially that posed by the moriscos, the forced Moslem converts to Christianity. In consequence of fear and alarm in government circles at the extension of Ottoman power across North Africa, conversion (or exile) was inflicted upon the Moors of Castile in 1502. This practice was extended to Valencia in 1525 and to Aragon in 1526, government policy being backed by the formidable apparatus of the Inquisition. An immediate result was the expulsion from Spain of a stream of bitterly resentful refugees, whose hatred of the government and knowledge of the country increased the number and effectiveness of Turkish and North African raids on the Spanish coastline. In the long term, the rulers of Spain were now forced to grapple with stubborn resistance to assimilation on the part of the recalcitrant morisco minority. In Valencia and Aragon the moriscos provided a substantial population of agricultural labourers whose industry and fertility made them an invaluable resource of the local aristocracy. In these regions government policy was consistently frustrated by the nobles who had every interest in protecting their prized labour force from external interference. When the moriscos of Valencia broke into revolt in 1526, the landlords of the region refused to cooperate in their suppression, the task being delegated by Madrid, at considerable trouble and expense, to specially imported contingents of German infantry.

It was, however, in the recently conquered kingdom of Granada, which contained a large Moorish population with its own governing class, that morisco resistance assumed the gravest proportions. The Moors were made restive and excited by reports of the spectacular exploits of the North African corsairs during the early 1560s. Tensions mounted during the siege of Malta in 1565, when many morisco refugees were prominent in the Turkish forces. Anxiety and suspicion hardened the customary brutality of official policy and provoked in 1568 a widespread morisco revolt. By 1569 the insurgents numbered over 150,000. The revolt coincided with a period of great difficulty for the government; the bulk of the army was absent with the Duke of Alba in the Netherlands, and naval patrols proved unable to cut the rebels off from their sources of encouragement and supply in Algiers. Only after a strenuous and barbaric campaign was the rebellion crushed in the autumn of 1570. The settlement imposed by the victorious government was typically unimaginative and severe: mass deportations, costly in life and suffering, of moriscos from Granada to the 'safe' provinces of Estremadura, Galicia and Old Castile. The effect was only to export the morisco problem into regions hitherto unaffected by it.

Troubles rankled on through the last decades of the sixteenth century. Further attempts were made to separate the moriscos from

77 The expulsion of the 'moriscos' from Spain (1609)

their North African allies by forbidding them access to maritime districts, those of Andalusia in 1579 and of Valencia in 1586. 'We must count all moriscos avowed enemies', reported a government official in 1588. Brutalized by harsh treatment, the moriscos dwindled in numbers and turned increasingly to crime and brigandage as a normal mode of life. In 1609 the government finally and formally admitted the bankruptcy of its policy and decreed the expulsion of all moriscos from Spain.

It seems clear that organization of resistance to Ottoman advance involved the Habsburg government of Spain in wasteful and un-creative activities which blighted the high hopes with which Charles V had entered upon his Iberian inheritance in 1516. Separatist and divisive social and political tendencies posed the major problem for Spain. The marriage of Ferdinand and Isabella marked the beginning of an attempt to pull the country together round its monarchy, but a prolonged period of patient and resolute administrative activity remained necessary if Spanish society was to be unified and articulated. The Mediterranean crusade against the Turks swallowed up the time, energy and finance essential to this enterprise. Distracted by the pressures and demands of war, the government was obliged to compromise with selfish and separatist interests, settling for a façade of unity, while leaving the deep domestic problems of the nation virtually untouched.

In the eighteenth century a Spanish civil servant wrote as follows of his country:

> A body composed of other and smaller bodies, separated and in opposition to one another, which oppress and despise each other and are in a continuous state of war. Each province, each religious house, each profession is separated from the rest of the nation and concentrated in itself . . . Modern Spain can be considered as a body without energy . . . a monstrous Republic formed of little republics which confront each other because the particular interest of each is in contradiction with the general interest.

The sterile and self-divided Spain of the eighteenth century was a consequence of opportunities lost during earlier periods. There is no single explanation for these failures of nerve and capacity; but much may be attributed to the crippling strain imposed upon the Spanish state and society in the sixteenth century by the long struggle against Islam in the Mediterranean.

ITALY

The chief animators, major beneficiaries and occasional victims of the growth of Spanish imperialism were the Italian bankers who spun the web of loans and contracts which enmeshed the whole enterprise. The intense and brilliant urban civilization of the late Middle Ages – Renaissance Italy – suffered irreparable damage during the early sixteenth century, when the peninsula was the battlefield of contending foreign powers, France, Spain and the Holy Roman Empire; but the constellation of Italian states still comprised the most complex and creative society in Europe.

The commercial and territorial colonies of the Italian trading republics in the Black Sea, the Balkans, the Aegean and the Levant brought Italians into early and frequently painful contact with the expanding Ottoman empire. In the sixteenth century, as the Turks consolidated their hold in the Balkans, conquered Syria and Egypt, allied with the North African pirate states and emerged as an aggressive sea power, Italy became increasingly exposed to Moslem attacks. Simultaneously – in part consequentially – much of the peninsula, Naples and Sicily, Genoa and Milan, was incorporated into the Spanish imperial system. With the Ottoman and Habsburg empires moving into conflict in the Mediterranean, Italy was placed in the front line of hostilities. Venice, Ancona, Messina, Naples, Leghorn and Genoa became the most sensitive points of European contact with the Ottoman world.

Two Italian states, Venice and Genoa, are selected here to provide specific illustration of the general Ottoman impact upon the social and economic systems of Italy. They differed greatly in their internal constitutions and political traditions. Venetian government was the unchallenged monopoly of an intelligent and implacable merchant aristocracy. Genoa was the theatre of ceaseless conflict between an aristocracy, whose wealth and power derived as much from banking and international trade as from feudal possessions and privileges, and the *popolo grasso*, the merchant and manufacturing middle class. By prudent diplomacy and the acquisition of a substantial *terra firma*, a broad belt of protective territory extending from Bergamo to the River Isonzo, Venice escaped the worst effects of the Italian wars of the early sixteenth century and remained independent of intrusive transalpine monarchies. Genoa, on the other hand, a strategic key to Italy for both France and Spain, was perpetually a protectorate of one or other of these contending great powers.

Both states were vulnerable to Turkish pressure; both suffered in consequence; and both were associated, not always willingly, with sixteenth-century resistance to the Ottomans under Spanish Habsburg leadership.

During and after the crusades, the Italian maritime republics insinuated themselves deeply into the economic life of south-eastern and Pontic Europe and the Middle East. Most acquired colonies in these areas, which were usually ports, like Genoese Caffa on the Black Sea, or islands, like Venetian Cyprus, administered by a proprietary class of Italian origin. They also planted important trading communities, frequently with negotiated rights of extra-territoriality, the most important being the Venetian settlements in Beirut and Alexandria and the Genoese quarter in Constantinople. Italian merchants shipped spices – pepper, cloves and ginger of Far Eastern origin – and silks from the ports of Syria and Egypt; alum and dried fruits from Asia Minor; oil and wine from the Greek islands; furs, tallow, dried fish and occasional slaves from Pontic Europe; and – in the case of Venice – grain from Moldavia, Wallachia, Macedonia and Cyprus.

The fifteenth- and sixteenth-century Ottoman conquests threatened these immensely profitable footholds. Venice was particularly vulnerable to Ottoman expansion. Her merchants dominated the spice trade, the Middle Eastern centres of which were incorporated into the Ottoman empire in 1516–17. Her wool textile industry found its largest market in the Levant. The food supply of the mother city depended on grain imports from areas which were now falling under Turkish control. To meet this crisis Venice disposed of

78 Procession of the *bailo*

formidable human and administrative resources. The Venetian government was the most rational and calculating in Europe, far advanced in the techniques of commerce, transportation, naval warfare, diplomacy and espionage. Venetian response and resistance to Ottoman pressure was characteristically cunning, complex and tenacious.

The republic whose rulers had been responsible in the early thirteenth century for the deflection of the Fourth Crusade into a predatory attack on the Byzantine empire found no difficulty, in the sixteenth, in rejecting a 'crusading' reaction to Ottoman expansion. To the Venetian government the growth of Ottoman power represented a grave problem but not an apocalyptic challenge. The Venetians exploited their capacity for being of frequent assistance to the Turks to win recognition and guarantee, often revoked but always restored, of their presence and commercial operations in Ottoman dominions. In 1533, for example, when the sultan proposed to attack the Italian possessions of Charles V, and was anxious to obtain details of Spanish counter-measures, he received Pietro Zeno, the Venetian ambassador at Constantinople, in audience with these words: 'Write immediately to your Signoria, for it can find out what the fish are doing at the bottom of the sea, and also about the

(Venetian ambassador to Constantinople) going to an audience with the sultan

fleet which Spain is preparing in her ports. Write immediately.' On this, as on other occasions, the Venetians proved obliging and unsentimental about exchanging information for economic concessions.

Venetian realism involved frank recognition that diplomacy alone could not sustain the position of the republic, which must often also be drawn into war against the aggressive Turks. The strategy adopted by the Venetian government was characteristically hard-headed and self-interested. It rested upon two principles: scientific fortification of important strongpoints in the overseas system to enable these to withstand long sieges; and, in the conduct of naval war, preference for brief but decisive campaigns, where the republic's relative poverty of material resources might be offset by the exercise of technical and organizational skills to produce spectacular victories from which an early resort to diplomacy might then extract the maximum advantage. The value of scientific fortification was

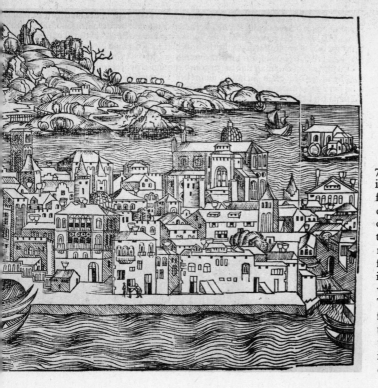

79 View of Venice in 1493. The fortunes of Venice depended on oriental trade, and, though the republic was frequently drawn into exhausting warfare against the Turks, merchants from the city clung tenaciously to their trading posts in the Ottoman dominions

illustrated in 1537, when the Turks were obliged to abandon the siege of Corfu after over-running the island but failing to reduce the Venetian fortresses before the onset of winter. Venice lost Euboea in 1470, but acquired Cyprus in 1489, and retained Crete, islands to the west of Greece and a string of colonies on the coasts of Dalmatia and the Morea. Only minor territorial losses were sustained prior to the Turkish capture of Cyprus in 1570. Crete was not lost until 1669, after a siege of twenty-four years; and when Ottoman power began finally to wane the Venetians were at hand to obtain most of the Morea by the Treaty of Karlowitz in 1699.

Attempts to implement a specifically Venetian naval strategy were evident during the wars of the late 1530s and again during the 1570s. At Prevesa in 1538 the Venetian captains were outraged by Andrea Doria's refusal to commit the allied fleet to battle. They were eager to exploit a rare opportunity for a quick victory over numerically inferior Turkish forces. Doria, by contrast, preoccupied with the

135

long-term defence of Spanish Italy and the western Mediterranean, was determined not to risk his fleet, which provided the only effective screen against Ottoman naval power, in pursuit of a problematic victory, which, even if it were achieved, could not be followed up by Spain. Similarly, later in the century, after contributing substantially to the victory of the Holy League at Lepanto in 1571, Venice became an increasingly unwilling partner in the alliance, from which she withdrew in 1573. With Cyprus lost and the economy of the republic strained by the war effort, the Venetian government was anxious to salvage what it could while the prestige obtained at Lepanto was at its height, rather than be dragged into an exhausting and unprofitable prolongation of the conflict.

Caught up in the great wars which reflected the simultaneous growth of Ottoman and Spanish imperialism, Venice was seldom able to impose this strategy decisively on the situation. When forced or manœuvred into lengthy campaigns against the Turks, she suffered severe territorial losses; Cyprus in the sixteenth century, Crete in the seventeenth. This raises the question of how far the economic decline of the republic, which was evident by the early seventeenth century, was a result of Ottoman expansion. Traditionally, historians have sought its origins elsewhere, stressing the effects upon the Venetian economy of the Portuguese discovery and exploitation of the Cape route to the spice centres of India and the Far East. Certainly there is evidence that this caused grave embarrassment to Venice, especially during the first decade of the sixteenth century; but the argument underestimates Venetian powers of endurance and recovery. The mid-sixteenth century witnessed a revival of the Middle Eastern traffic in spices. During the 1560s Alexandria was receiving consignments of pepper at least equal to those which were arriving at Lisbon. That Venice continued to profit from this commerce is shown by the fact that the *fondaco* or colony of south German merchants resident in the city, whose principal interests lay in organizing the supply of spices to central Europe, paid over 40,000 ducats in taxes to the republic during 1561-2, as compared with the 18,000 ducats paid in 1490, before the opening of the Cape route. There is much other evidence to support the view that historians have tended to pre-date Venetian economic decadence. Pierre Sardella has shown that the shipbuilding, ceramics, sugar-refining, printing and glass-working industries of the city all expanded throughout the sixteenth century. Population also rose on a healthy curve, from 115,000 in 1509 to 168,000 in 1563.

Yet by the early seventeenth century evidence of decline was clear and unmistakable. This was particularly true of the manufacture and export of woollen textiles, which was of central importance in the economy of the republic and one of its principal outlets into the Ottoman world. In 1612 the English ambassador to Venice reported:

> even the commodities of this cities which were wont to be carried into Soria fayle likewise of vent, insomuch that for some years past there was 24,000 and 25,000 clothes sent thether a year. This last year 1611 there was but 15,000 and the next it is not thought there will be above 10,000 or 12,000.

Contemporary Venetian documents provide copious confirmation of this verdict, and also, significantly, assign ultimate responsibility for the situation to involvement in the War of Cyprus, 1570–3. The loss of Cyprus deprived Venice of an important grain and wine producing centre and a regular port of call for galleys *en route* to Syrian and Egyptian ports. But this was only one episode in a chain of disasters. Simultaneously, Venice was cut off for several years from her normal sources of grain supply and injured by the interruption of eastern trade. Commerce was crippled by the soaring costs of marine insurance during a period when the Mediterranean was the theatre of intensive naval operations. The capacities of the Venetian arsenal were seriously strained by the task of providing and maintaining warships for the Christian fleet which triumphed at Lepanto. In 1573 English merchants re-entered the Mediterranean after an absence of more than twenty years. Disposing of large quantities of cheap cloth and trading from sailing ships which were faster, safer and more capacious than Venetian galleys, they were to prove formidable rivals. By 1612 twenty English business houses were established in Constantinople, while the Venetian depôts had

137

dwindled to five. As Venetian commentators pointed out, the English were attracted back into a Mediterranean world where the wasting wars between Spain and the Turks had stimulated a demand, most evident in the Ottoman dominions, for cloth, foodstuffs and metals (especially tin for casting cannon).

Above all, during and after the War of Cyprus, Venetian shipping was mercilessly harried by both Christian and Moslem corsairs, whose activities were enormously expanded by the collision of Spanish with Ottoman imperialism. Corsairs were the irregular troops of large-scale naval warfare, cheap and easy to raise, difficult to disband; quick to prey, when peace was concluded, on the weakest of the 'respectable' powers. The Venetian economy had always been acutely sensitive to piracy; as early as 1501 the news that a celebrated Turkish corsair, Kemali, was operating in the Aegean produced an instantaneous rise in the cost of marine insurance from two per cent to a prohibitive ten per cent. But only as a result of the conflict between Spain and the Turks was this problem to assume unmanageable proportions. The cessation of formal hostilities between the great powers of the Mediterranean during the 1580s intensified the piracy which these hostilities had stimulated. The French ambassador at Venice in 1607 reported: 'Cette place est tellement affligée par le danger des corsaires que la plupart des artisans, tant de soye que de laine, ne font plus rien.' His English colleague added in 1612:

> these signori are much condemned of incuriousness for not providing some sufficient convoy or setting out some vessels purposely against the *corsari* which they never took into consideration, as if therein they had lost their judgements.

The most severe depredations on Venetian shipping were carried out by the uskoks, refugee Serbs and Bosnians settled by the Austrian Habsburgs in Carniola, whose operations eventually compelled the republic to undertake the ruinously expensive *guerra di uscocchi* in the Adriatic from 1614 to 1617.

Of course, Venetian economic decline was not a simple function of Ottoman expansion, nor did everything stem from the events of the early 1570s. Other factors must be taken into account, notably the adverse effects of excessive *dirigismo* on Venetian industry. The Venetian government, intent on the prevention of fratricidal economic competition among its citizens, created a jungle of regulations which stifled enterprise and inhibited innovation. It is nevertheless impossible to escape the general conclusion that as an historical episode the rundown of the Venetian economy was governed and dictated by the sixteenth-century explosion of Ottoman power and the European reaction to it.

While Ottoman aggression forced Venice down the road to ruin, it conferred prosperity on Genoa. This was not immediately apparent. The eastern outposts of Genoa capitulated to Ottoman invaders much more rapidly than those of Venice. Phocaea, the alum-producing centre in Asia Minor, was lost in 1452. Genoese merchants were closely associated with the Byzantine empire, both in the metropolis and in the Black Sea trading area, and their prosperity collapsed with the capture of Constantinople. Caffa and other ports in the Black Sea fell to the Turks in 1475. In the Aegean, Imbros, Lemnos and Samothrace were lost in 1456, and Lesbos surrendered in 1462. The sole remaining outpost, the rich island of Chios, survived until 1566, when it was seized and sacked by the Turks in an outburst of bad temper following their defeat at Malta in the previous year.

The Genoese never mounted a resilient and resourceful rearguard action on the Venetian model. The Ligurian republic, notorious for the fiercely competitive individualism of its commercial and political life, had no comparable resources of patriotism on which to draw. From the fourteenth to the sixteenth century Genoa was distracted by bitter faction fights between the ancient nobility and the *popolo grasso*. The latter won control of the government in 1339 and, through wealthy and powerful families like those of Sauli and Giustiniani, dominated the city's eastern trade. During the fifteenth century, as this commerce dwindled under increasing Ottoman pressure, an aristocratic reaction gathered strength in home affairs. This derived from the creation in 1407 of an association of predominantly aristocratic state creditors, the Bank of St George. Mounting commitments and continuing losses in the Black Sea and the Middle East plunged the middle-class government into chronic financial difficulties which it was able to meet only at the cost of alienating territory and farming taxes to the Bank in return for loans. In the early sixteenth century an astute Florentine observer, Niccolò Machiavelli, noted the significance of this development, suggesting that the nobility, by engrossing so large a share of the administration in a period when the government was plagued by factional strife and wilting under foreign aggression, might eventually take over the state. The Ligurian aristocracy, in short, through control of public finance, were infiltrating back into political power.

Domestic divisions were therefore a prime cause of the failure of Genoa to offer determined and concerted resistance to Ottoman conquest. A further explanation lay in the prodigious opportunities which arose in the late fifteenth and early sixteenth centuries of obtaining compensation in the west for commercial and territorial losses sustained at the hands of the Turks. The collapse of the com-mercial-colonial empire in the Black Sea and the Levant occasioned a massive reorientation of the economy of the republic by the foundation of a commercial-financial empire in the rising Iberian kingdoms and their dependencies. At its point of fullest development, during the late sixteenth century, this structure differed in three respects from the empire which had been lost to the Turks: it was entirely economic, not territorial in character; it concentrated primarily, though never exclusively, on finance and contracting rather than routine commerce; and it was the creation of the Ligurian aristocracy who overthrew and replaced the *popolo grasso* as the ruling class of the republic in 1528.

As Portugal prospered during the fifteenth century, representatives of aristocratic Genoese business houses, Doria, Centurione, Cattaneo, Salvago, Spinola, drifted to Lisbon. By 1500 they dominated the sugar trade, owning plantations and refineries in Madeira and the Azores, exporting the product via Lisbon to Genoa, and marketing throughout southern and central Europe. But it was into the economy of an emergent and expansive Spain that the Genoese, thrown back from the Levant, burrowed most successfully. Investigations in the notarial archives of Seville have shown how, as secret shareholders in Spanish trading houses, as money-lenders and as marine insurance agents, they were the principal mediators in the commerce between Spain and the New World between 1502 and 1520. The Mediterranean dependencies of the Spanish monarchy, Sardinia and the Two Sicilies, became honeycombed with Genoese commercial colonies during the late fifteenth and the early sixteenth centuries. In metropolitan Spain the Castilian Cortes of 1528 complained that the trade in wool, silk, steel and soap was being monopolized by the Genoese.

The pace of economic penetration was quickened in that year when the Genoese admiral Andrea Doria deserted with his navy from the service of France to that of Spain and simultaneously established aristocratic political control in his native republic. The resources of the *popolo grasso* shrank with the loss of the eastern colonies while those of the aristocracy expanded as a result of their Spanish investments. Protection and preservation of the latter dictated a Spanish alliance. Doria's *coup d'état* brought the political arrangements of the republic into abrupt conformity with economic reality. As bullion imports from the Americas to Seville assumed tidal proportions, stimulating the rapid growth of Spanish imperialism, so the numbers and activities of Genoese financiers increased in Spain. During the 1550s they outdistanced most of their German and Florentine rivals. In 1558 the firm of Grimaldi advanced one million gold *scudi* in a single loan to the Spanish crown. Loans such as these were made at high rates of interest; between ten and fourteen per cent was calculated on long-standing debts. Creditors received territorial grants, titles, monopolies of trade and manufacture and privileges of tax farming if the crown defaulted on its payments. In face of such transactions the Cortes of 1542 and 1592 repeated the protests made in 1528 about Genoese parasitism on the Spanish economy. To no avail; in 1595 it was calculated that of the precious metals imported into Spain during the preceding sixty-four years the equivalent of 24 million ducats had gone directly to the Genoese in repayment of loans.

The creation by Andrea Doria of firm and formal links between
Genoa and Spain and the pressing Spanish need for warships to
undertake the burden of maritime defence against the Turks opened
considerable opportunities in the field of naval contracting. The navy
of Italy under Doria's command was the guarantee of Charles V's
supremacy in the peninsula and the first defence of Christendom
against Moslem attack. The nucleus of this fleet was provided by
galleys which were Doria's personal property on hire to Spain. He
was already an important naval contractor, the proprietor of a dozen
galleys, when he joined Charles V in 1528. He owned thirty-nine
by 1552.

The circulation of these galleys dictated the whole rhythm and
respiration of the Spanish Mediterranean war effort against the
Turks in the critical middle years of the sixteenth century. Doria
was responsible for organizing the necessary peregrinations of
Charles V between Spain and Italy. He provided the shipping, the
sailors, the convoy vessels and the harbour facilities of Liguria. The
movements of Charles alone, omitting the ceaseless comings and
goings of subordinates, illustrate the importance of Doria's role as
a ferryman: 1529, Palamos to Savona; 1533, Genoa to Barcelona;

80, 81 View of Genoa in the sixteenth century.
The Genoese Gian-Andrea Doria (above) succeeded
his uncle Andrea as Grand-Admiral of Spain

1536, Genoa to Barcelona; 1538, Genoa to Aigues-Mortes to Barcelona; 1541, Genoa to Spezia to Algiers; 1543, Barcelona to Savona to Genoa.

Troop transportation was another heavy task undertaken by Doria's galleys. In 1550, when his fleet touched at Naples *en route* to attack the corsair base of Mahedia in North Africa, it carried 20,000 Spanish soldiers. Later in the same year, off the North African coast, he detached twenty-four galleys to fetch siege guns and infantry reinforcements from Italy. During a naval action at Terracina in 1552 the Turks took seven of Doria's galleys filled with troops. In 1559, when the Spanish expedition against Dragut's outpost at Djerba was assembling, his nephew, Gian-Andrea Doria, sent galleys to transport some thousands of German and Italian infantry from Genoa to Messina.

Other members of the Ligurian nobility, notably the families of Negrone, Imperiale, Grimaldi, Usodimare and Cigala, followed Doria's lead in this specialism. The fleet which Gian-Andrea Doria led into action at Djerba in 1560 included, in addition to his uncle's large contingent, thirteen galleys constructed and hired out by Genoese contractors.

143

Bearing in mind this remarkable record of financial and economic parasitism, it comes as no surprise to discover the Genoese portrayed as bloodsuckers in Spanish political and satirical literature of the sixteenth and early seventeenth centuries. Yet these parasites nourished as well as debilitated their hosts. It is difficult to imagine how the ponderous and elaborate Habsburg system could have been built up to a point where it was capable of sustaining and repelling Ottoman attacks without the financial and administrative skills provided by the business and sea-faring aristocracy of Liguria.

By abandoning their traditional commercial interests in the eastern Mediterranean and the Black Sea for the new role of principal animators of Spanish imperialism, the Genoese were therefore still operating in a context created by the sixteenth-century expansion of Ottoman power. For it was the Turkish menace which obliged and enabled Charles V to breathe fresh life into the moribund imperial idea. And it was the Turkish menace which reconciled the Italians to the prospect of political dominion by the Emperor and his successors.

Just as Ottoman absorption of their commercial colonies in the Aegean and the Black Sea originally impelled the Genoese to transfer their business interests in the direction of the Iberian powers, so, later, the furious Turkish and North African naval offensive against Mediterranean Europe, which began with Barbarossa's exploits in the 1540s and reached a climax during the 1560s, dictated developments which enabled Genoese financiers to confirm and extend the indispensable role which they had come to play in the economy of Spain. Through most of the sixteenth century the bulk of Spanish American bullion, the essential source and guarantee of Spanish greatness, was customarily shipped after its passage across the Atlantic from Seville to the Netherlands. From Antwerp it then circulated throughout northern, western and central Europe in exchange for the goods and services which upheld the Spanish system.

From the early 1570s an alternative route came into increasing use. American precious metals were now transported across the Mediterranean in galleys from Barcelona to Genoa. The Ligurian city rapidly replaced Antwerp as the major distribution centre for

Spanish silver and thus as the financial capital of Europe. Utilization of this new route corresponds and connects with the great Mediterranean naval wars provoked by increasing Ottoman pressure and particularly with the exertions of the Holy League during the 1570s. The Spanish empire was diverting its most valuable resources towards the scene of its most strenuous efforts. This conferred upon Genoa a strategic position in the economy not only of imperial Spain but of all southern and Mediterranean Europe; a position which was maintained until the flood of Spanish American bullion began to decline in the third decade of the seventeenth century.

EUROPEAN CONSCIOUSNESS OF THE TURK

The impression of the Turks current among sixteenth-century Europeans varied from class to class and from country to country. We have seen how the Turks were frequently welcomed as liberators by Balkan peasants and Greek islanders. But these were populations belonging to cultures which were already half eastern in character, habituated over generations to the proximity of the Ottoman empire and subject to severe economic exploitation by their European masters. Echoes of their readiness to accept Ottoman rule were heard in some towns of mainland Italy, in Ancona in 1480 and in Ravenna during the early sixteenth century, when a deputy from the city told Cardinal Giulio Medici, the papal legate: 'Monsignore, if the Turk comes to Ragusa we will put ourselves in his hands.' This was a desperate final resort of medieval communal patriotism in face of the centralizing policy of the Renaissance popes.

In general, as one moved westwards into the heartlands of European society, the Ottomans became increasingly the object of loathing and fear. The apparently irresistible progress of their arms contributed to the profound and superstitious pessimism which marked the popular psychology of the age. Of course other factors contributed to the development of this morbid sensibility, particularly the incidence in Europe of syphilis and plague and the atmosphere of hell-fire revivalism which was both a cause and consequence of the Reformation. It was, indeed, as a crowning tribulation willed by a wrathful God upon backsliding Christian peoples that Martin

Luther, who knew better than most how to play on the fears and
bewilderment of a mass audience, pictured the Turks in his *War
Sermon* of 1529. He saw them as fulfilling the prophecy of Ezekiel
('Satan will be loosed from his prison') and the Revelation of St
John ('Behold, I . . . will bring a sword upon you . . . I will bring
the worst of the nations to take possession of their homes'). Popular
apprehensions were not so strong in remote and sheltered northern
and western Europe, though even in these regions crusading propaganda was still capable of striking a deep response. But among the
peasants of Germany and central Europe the Ottoman menace
produced an endemic 'Great Fear'.

The reaction of many influential and articulate men was equally
emotional. Authors and clerics revived and refurbished the diatribes
against the infidel which had characterized the period of the crusades.
The Turks, it was argued, were beyond the pale, not merely of
Christianity but of civilization itself. Cardinal Bessarion, writing
to the Doge of Venice after the fall of Constantinople, set the tone
for a century of abuse:

A city which was so flourishing . . . the splendour and glory of
the East . . . the refuge of all good things, has been captured,
despoiled, ravaged and completely sacked by the most inhuman
barbarians . . . by the fiercest of wild beasts . . . Much danger
threatens Italy, not to mention other lands, if the violent
assaults of the most ferocious barbarians are not checked.

The tradition was maintained and extended to a popular audience
during the sixteenth century by the crude war propaganda of
Bartholomew Georgevich of Croatia, whose best-selling *Miseries and
Tribulations of the Christians held in Tribute and Slavery by the Turks*
(1544) appeared in many editions and numerous languages.

From the unpromising breeding-ground of this vehement
rejection of the Turks, an important new perspective was to emerge.
Medieval writers had been able, with no sense of absurdity, to
envisage 'the World's Debate' as a conflict between Islam on the
one hand and the 'common corps of Christendom' on the other.
'Christendom' had always been a term more expressive of ideals
and aspirations than of realities. The political and religious developments of the fifteenth and sixteenth centuries finally drained it of
significance. Not only was the term empty; worse, it was embarrass-
ing. Elementary political realism made it necessary for some
Christian powers, such as France or the frontier states of eastern
Europe, to negotiate and occasionally make alliance with the Turks.
Continued stress on the concept of Christendom, implying an

obligation to assume an attitude of total hostility to the infidel, was incompatible with such actions.

Yet the fact remained that the Ottoman empire seemed different in kind from other states. War against the Turks, for example, was felt to belong to a different category of conflict from other wars, which were mere family quarrels over titles, territory or Biblical interpretation. It was, in the phrase of James VI of Scotland, battle joined in 'the public cause'. A lawyer's version of the same point was advanced by the Elizabethan jurist, Alberico Gentili, who argued in his *De iure belli* (1588–9) that, though infidel and Christian communities were bound together in a common *societas gentium*, so that war between them could not be natural, it was nevertheless 'almost natural' by reason of the insatiable aggressiveness of the Turks: 'we constantly have a legitimate reason for war against the Turk'. Whatever contacts might be dictated by political necessity, the Turks were still an object of profound suspicion and distrust.

The difficulty remained that if Christendom was a dead – or dying – focus of loyalty and support, surviving only in sermons or the preambles to international treaties, what was 'the public cause'? The answer which emerged haltingly over a full century of discussion and debate was that it was the cause of *Europe*. Until the fifteenth century 'Europe' remained a neutral geographical expression. Then, as Ottoman attacks increased in severity, Polish and Habsburg publicists began to suggest that their governments were defending not merely European territory but also specifically European values against Moslem aggression. The notion became fashionable in humanist and literary circles. The Italian poets Ariosto and Tasso used the word 'Europe' to imply a unique social and value system as well as a geographical area. Erasmus exhorted 'the nations of Europe' – no longer addressing them as the constituent powers of Christendom – to a crusade against the Turks. Indulging his imagination, the French poet Ronsard proposed in 1555 that Europe might be saved by abandoning European territory to the Ottomans and transporting European societies *in toto* to the New World, where they could preserve their values and resume their development unhindered by Moslem attacks.

This transition from 'Christendom' to 'Europe', from a religious to a secular term of identification, did not involve the elimination of the Christian element. Profession of the Christian faith was still a necessary – and in the eyes of most people much the most important – part of being a European. The real extent of the change can perhaps best be conveyed by recalling the title of the first volume in the series of which this book forms a part. Professor Trevor-Roper's theme was *The Rise of Christian Europe*. Turkish pressure during the late fifteenth and the sixteenth centuries stimulated a process of self-examination which led members of the societies concerned increasingly to identify themselves and to distinguish themselves from the Ottoman enemy by reference to the second rather than the first term of Professor Trevor-Roper's equation.

One of the factors which made it difficult for men in the sixteenth century to subscribe to the concept of 'the common corps of Christendom' was the Reformation, which dissolved Christian society into a multitude of warring sects. Since Catholic powers under Habsburg leadership were in the forefront of European resistance to the Turks, one might have expected Protestants to view the Ottomans more benignly. There is little evidence that this was so. Certainly Elizabeth I of England entered into close diplomatic relations with Constantinople; but so, much earlier in the sixteenth century, had The Most Christian King Francis I of France. The Queen's ecclesiastical officials exemplified a more enduring Protestant attitude. In 1565 Bishop Jewel of Salisbury ordered prayers to be said throughout his diocese for the relief of Malta. When news arrived that the island was saved, Archbishop Parker of Canterbury ordered prayers of thanksgiving. This Protestant response is not really surprising. When, for instance, in 1528 Luther called on Charles V to unite Germany in a war against the Turks, one suspects that the consideration was not altogether absent from his mind that such an enterprise might divert the attention of emperor and pope from the business of persecuting Protestants. A hard-bitten Elizabethan Protestant politician, Sir Francis Walsingham, made such calculations explicit and carried them a stage further. He viewed the conflict of Catholic and Ottoman in the Mediterranean as a struggle

149

between 'two limbs of the devil', and hoped that it would end in mutual extermination. But he did not express this view publicly. Another Elizabethan minister, Sir Robert Cecil, was much closer to the standard Protestant opinion: 'in Christianity I may not wish a Heathen prosperity'. Thomas Fuller, in the seventeenth century, probably best expressed the nice combination of high-mindedness, self-interest and complacency which characterized the Protestant position. In *The Historie of the Holy Warre* (1639) he praised the King of Spain:

> Yea, all West-Christendom oweth her quiet sleep to his constant waking, who with his galleys muzzleth the mouth of Tunis and Algiers. Yea, God in his Providence hath so ordered it, that the dominions of Catholic princes . . . are the case and corner of the east and south to keep and fence the Protestant countries.

A small number of level-headed commentators refused to join in the general chorus of European denunciation of the Turks. Most of these were diplomats who had crossed the frontiers of the Ottoman world and seen for themselves, or scholars capable of making a dispassionate study of the development and structure of the Turkish empire. Notable among them was Ogier Ghiselin de Busbecq, Imperial ambassador at Constantinople from 1554 to 1562, who wrote with open admiration of the Ottoman military and administrative system:

> It is by merit that men rise in the service, a system which ensures that posts should be assigned only to the competent . . . Those who receive the highest offices from the Sultan are for the most part the sons of shepherds or herdsmen, and so far from being ashamed of their parentage, they actually glory in it, and consider it a matter for boasting that they owe nothing to the accident of birth; for they do not believe that high qualities are either natural or hereditary, nor do they think that they can be handed down from father to son, but that they are partly the gift of God, and partly the result of good training, great

industry, and unwearied zeal . . . Among the Turks, therefore, honours, high posts, and judgeships are the rewards of great ability and good service . . .

This is the reason that they are successful in their undertakings, that they lord it over others, and are daily extending the bounds of their empire. These are not our ideas, with us there is no opening left for merit; birth is the standard for everything; the prestige of birth is the sole key to advancement in the public service.

Machiavelli had accustomed Europeans to regard war as a natural relationship between states and to venerate the martial practices of the ancients. His humanist successors singled out Ottoman military arrangements for special praise. Paolo Giovio in his *Turcicarum Rerum Commentarius* of 1539 wrote: 'Their military discipline has such justice and severity as easily to surpass the ancient Greeks and Romans.'

In contrast, it was the quality of Ottoman civil administration which impressed the French diplomat, Philippe du Fresne-Canaye. The sultan, he wrote in his *Voyage du Levant* (1573):

gouverne de telle façon tant de peuples si divers de langue, de religion et de coutume, qu'il semble que tout son empire ne soit qu'une seule et même cité, tant est grande la paix et l'obéissance qui règne dans toutes ses parties.

For Jean Bodin, whose *Six Books of the Republic* (1576) was composed during the bitterest phase of the French Wars of Religion, toleration was the chief Turkish claim to admiration and respect:

The King of the Turks, who rules over a great part of Europe, safeguards the rites of religion as well as any prince in this world. Yet he constrains no one, but on the contrary permits everyone to live according as his conscience dictates. What is more, even in his seraglio at Pera he permits the practice of four diverse religions, that of the Jews, the Christian according to the Roman rite, and according to the Greek rite, and that of Islam.

There are elements of exaggeration and misinformation in these panegyrics. Commentators like Busbecq and Bodin were perhaps more concerned to promote reforms at home than to provide a wholly accurate picture of Ottoman customs. They represented, nevertheless, an important section of minority opinion which refused to be stampeded into conventional hysterical abuse. Sustaining this rational attitude was a growing body of scholarly writing about the Turkish empire. Sixteenth-century Europeans were much more eager for information on this subject than for similar studies of the New World. In France alone there appeared between 1480 and 1609 over eighty books on Turkey as compared with forty titles concerning the Americas. Some contributions to this European literature, notably the wide-ranging philological explorations of the great but eccentric French orientalist Guillaume Postel and the Italian Francesco Sansovino's *Historia universale del origine e imperio de' Turchi*, published at Venice in 1568, were of the highest quality. The intelligent curiosity displayed in works such as these, unreciprocated from the Ottoman side, was to prove in the long run a better guarantee of Europe's capacity to resist and overcome the Turks than the intolerant fanaticism of propagandists and pamphleteers.

85, 86 The Italian humanist Paolo Giovio (far left) and the Flemish diplomat Busbecq (left)

87, 88 The title-page of Thomas Fuller's *Historie of the Holy Warre* (left) is a Protestant parable on the spiritual pride and material waste of crusading against the infidel. The Moslem mind was less afflicted by self-doubt or scruple. Note the blank spaces for sons or brothers assassinated during or immediately after the succession struggles in the picturesque genealogy (above) of the Ottoman sultans

All empires are to some extent plunder machines, but few have matched the thoroughness and deliberation with which the Ottomans pursued this objective. And in none has the assimilation and employment of alien manpower been carried to such lengths. The child tribute of the Balkans and the slave raids of the Crimean Tartars into Poland and the Ukraine provided the Turkish empire with its finest soldiers and administrators. The imperial harem was recruited from the same sources. Khurrem, the favourite wife of Suleiman the Magnificent and mother of Selim II, was a South Russian. Selim II's favourite consort came from a Greek family of Corfu. The appetite of the Ottoman empire for human plunder remained unsatisfied by the tribute of the conquered provinces and the borderlands. Constantinople also attracted and made use of a stream of renegades and refugees from the European states with which it was in conflict.

Historians properly stress the extent to which sixteenth-century Europe was local in its roots and anchorage. Certainly the mass of cultivators and artisans seldom moved beyond their familiar locations. But a number of factors – the inflation caused by the influx of Spanish American bullion; religious persecution; a growing international market for the specialized skills of the printer, the shipwright and the miner; the crude demand for cannon fodder in an age of great wars – conspired to produce a numerous class of rootless, socially disinherited men, who were prepared to cross the racial and, if necessary, the religious frontier in pursuit of profit and power. The Ottoman world exercised a strong influence upon such people. The Turks practised a high degree of religious toleration, whereas European governments did not. The Turkish military and economic systems provided men of obscure origin with avenues of rapid social and political advancement, whereas Europe did not. The Ottoman empire was a lavish provider of booty for daring and resourceful employees. This attractive power was recognized and understood by European contemporaries. Martin Luther appealed with special force to those of his countrymen who found themselves, by whatever chance, captives in Turkish hands, to resist what he admitted to be the strong temptation to become renegades.

Formal conversion was necessary if a man was to rise high in Ottoman public life. Once this step had been taken, prospects were limited only by luck and natural ability. In 1573 a French nobleman, Philippe du Fresne-Canaye, accompanied the ambassador, François de Noailles, to Constantinople. It was a time of great interest and activity. The Turks were completing the restoration of the fleet which had been decimated at Lepanto two years before. Du Fresne was present at a review of the new fleet before its departure to action stations in the Aegean. From his account it is evident that the master planner was the Grand Vizier, Mehemet Sokolli, himself a slave of Bosnian Christian origins. The details of constructing, provisioning and manning the galleys were entrusted to the newly appointed Grand Admiral or 'Pasha of the Sea', Ucchiali, sometime Viceroy of Algiers. When the armada sailed it was commanded by Piali, the 'Second Pasha'. The rearguard squadron was commanded by Hassan Aga, treasurer and paymaster of the fleet. Ucchiali was a Calabrian, Piali a Hungarian and Hassan a Venetian renegade. These were figures of the great world. Setting out on their sea voyage home, du Fresne and his companions met a renegade of less exalted status. Detained during their passage through the Dardanelles by the Turkish garrison at Gallipoli, they were, in return for a generous bribe, conducted through the maze of corrupt Ottoman officialdom by a 'spahi, Espagnol renégat'.

To 'turn Turk' did not necessarily mean the end of all friendly contact with one's homeland. The correspondence, preserved in the State Archives of Genoa, of Battista Ferrari, 'agent' of the republic in Constantinople from 1562 to 1567, includes for the year 1564 alone detailed reports on Ottoman diplomatic activity and naval preparations from 'Mocat Aga', 'Mostaffa Rais' and 'Ferrato Beij', all three renegade Genoese in the sultan's service. Some renegades returned to Europe after a period in Ottoman pay. In compiling his account of Ottoman affairs, the sixteenth-century Italian historian Paolo Giovio drew considerably on evidence provided by returned and disillusioned renegades. Giovanni Antonio Menavino, an Italian who had served Sultan Bayazid as a page, gave him information concerning the circumstances of his late master's death in 1512.

89 Gracia Nasi,
matriarch of a Jewish family
that settled
in Constantinople

Giovio's account of the siege of Gran in Hungary in 1543 was based upon conversations with four Spanish renegades who deserted from the Turkish army before the fortress.

Refugees provided a second stream of European emigration into Turkish society. The moriscos, the forcibly converted Moorish New Christians of Spain, fled in considerable numbers to the North African pirate kingdoms. But the most important refugee group was that of the Iberian Jews. The career of one of these, Joseph Nasi, is worth following in some detail, illustrating as it does the prominent role which talented and ambitious aliens could aspire to play in Ottoman affairs.

The religious bigotry of the Iberian powers found expression during the late fifteenth century in a policy of expulsion and enforced conversion. Joseph Nasi was born about 1520 into a family of Jewish merchants and physicians who were expelled from Spain in 1492 and underwent forcible conversion in Lisbon in 1497. The establishment of the Inquisition in Portugal in 1536 decided the widowed matriarch, Gracia Nasi, to remove the entire family, including Joseph, her nephew and future son-in-law, to Antwerp. Joseph became a wealthy and respected businessman, well-known and well-received at the courts of France, the Habsburg Netherlands and Italy. He was knighted by Charles V and befriended by Charles' nephew, the future Emperor Maximilian II. A revival of racial prejudice and increasing suspicion that the Christian professions of the Nasi family were more formal than sincere obliged them to migrate to Venice in 1544, from Venice to Ferrara in 1552 and, finally, to escape the prospect of extremely harsh persecution, to Constantinople in 1553. Joseph Nasi joined them there in 1554 and immediately declared himself a convert to Judaism. In the years which followed he became famous as a merchant specializing in the wine trade, as a trusted diplomatic adviser to the Ottoman government and as a lavish patron of Hebrew literary circles in Constantinople and Salonika. Turkish documents of the time refer to him as *Frenk Bey Oglu* ('Frankish Prince'); to the citizens of Constantinople he was simply 'The Great Jew'. A period of considerable influence and power opened with the accession of his friend and patron Selim II to the throne in 1566. Selim named him Duke of Naxos, a fief which comprised a cluster of a dozen Aegean islands of considerable commercial and some strategic importance. He built up a network of diplomatic and commercial contacts in Poland, Moldavia and Wallachia. Selim later granted him the monopoly of wine imports to Constantinople. At court he was a prominent member of the war party which maintained the tradition of Khair-redin Barbarossa, preaching ceaseless hostility against all Catholic Mediterranean powers. He aspired to the throne of Cyprus when Ottoman forces invaded the island in 1570.

Joseph Nasi's influence waned after the conclusion of peace with Venice in 1573 and the death of Selim in 1574, when he retired to a life of what his biographer, Cecil Roth, calls 'gilded obscurity' in his palace of Belvedere on the Bosphorus. His role of courtier, businessman and foreign policy adviser was promptly assumed by another Jew, a refugee of German origin, Solomon Nathan Ashkenazi, *Allaman Oglu* to Turkish chroniclers. But the tide of Ottoman favour was running out for European Jewish refugees. Paths of advancement remained open to some, but spasmodic, sometimes extremely savage persecution made the life of the Jewish refugee communities in Ottoman territory increasingly insecure. Their ascendancy had depended on two advantages which they brought with them to Constantinople: continuing contacts with friends, relations and commercial agents scattered throughout Europe which made them a unique source of information in the power struggle of Turkey against Spain; and possession of certain technical and financial skills which were scarce in Ottoman society but necessary to sustain the cumbrous administrative structure of a great empire. As the years passed, the closeness of their European contacts and hence the accuracy and reliability of their information deteriorated. Simultaneously, in the great towns and the agricultural supply centres of the empire Greek merchants of Orthodox Christian faith challenged and during the seventeenth century overthrew the Jewish monopoly of banking and money-lending. The Jewish community declined into subordinate status as craftsmen, shopkeepers, pawn-brokers and quack doctors. The subject peoples of the Balkans were acquiring for themselves the skills which had enabled refugees of European origin to perform in the Ottoman empire during the second half of the sixteenth century a role similar to that which was played in the same period by the Genoese in the economic life and Mediterranean naval operations of imperial Spain.

90 Jewish doctor. Jews were in considerable demand as physicians in the Ottoman as in the European world in the sixteenth century, but it was as financiers and business agents that they were most influential at Constantinople during this period

V THE BEGINNING OF THE END

The preoccupation of European powers with dynastic and religious rivalries during the first half of the sixteenth century undoubtedly contributed to the dramatic sweep and scale of Ottoman conquest. Conversely, the success of Europeans in patching up some of their most violent quarrels during the middle years of the century helped to produce the strategic deadlock between the Ottomans and the Habsburgs on the Danube which was confirmed by the experience of Suleiman the Magnificent's last Hungarian campaign. The Peace of Augsburg in 1555 called a halt to nearly forty years of bitter religious conflict in the Holy Roman Empire. The Treaty of Cateau-Cambrésis in 1559 ended the long dynastic struggle between the Habsburgs and the Valois monarchy of France. Released, at least for the time being, from two of their major entanglements, the Austrian Habsburgs were able to devote more time and resources to the defence of the eastern European frontier against the Turks.

But in the second decade of the seventeenth century Germany and central Europe experienced a revival of political and religious controversy which culminated in 1618 in the outbreak of the Thirty Years War. Many contemporaries warned that these disturbances invited a repetition in some of the most vulnerable regions of Europe of the catastrophes which had overtaken the Serbian and Byzantine empires and the kingdom of Hungary in previous centuries, with Ottoman armies driving now into the heart of Europe. This was not to happen. The convulsions in Germany coincided with internal stresses in the Ottoman empire which were of such severity as to render the Turks incapable of taking advantage of the situation.

Yet European hopes that the Ottoman empire was decadent and the age of Turkish aggression at an end proved to be exaggerated. Ottoman statesmen of exceptional energy and intelligence were still capable of arresting and, to some extent, even reversing the

159

processes of decline. The middle years of the seventeenth century saw signs of recovery and a renewal of Ottoman advance. By 1676 the Turkish frontiers in Europe were more extensive than ever. In 1683 an Ottoman army laid siege for a second time to Vienna.

These successes, however, were partial and transient. The optimism of Europeans may have been premature, but it was justified in the long run. Driven back from Vienna, the Turks were subjected to a long series of military defeats by the Imperialists in Hungary, Serbia and Bosnia and by the Venetians in Dalmatia and the Morea. Utterly overthrown at the Battle of Zenta in 1697, they were obliged to sue for peace and to accept the hard terms of the Treaty of Karlowitz in 1699. The Ottoman empire remained a great power in Europe, retaining the whole length of the lower Danube from its Black Sea outlets to its confluence with the Drava north of Belgrade. These possessions were to be stubbornly defended over centuries. But the elementary, tidal force of Turkish conquest had ebbed and subsided; 'The World's Debate' had resolved itself into The Eastern Question.

91 The reign (1566–74) of Selim II, 'the Sot', who was more interested in bottles than battles, saw the beginning of a marked decline in the energy and capacity for leadership of the Ottoman sultans

92 In 1683 as in 1529 the flood-tide of Ottoman conquest broke against the defences of Vienna. This near-contemporary Austrian painting shows a fierce engagement outside the palisades which surrounded the city ▶

It is no longer fashionable for historians to stress the importance of individual human personality in the historical process. This book, with its emphasis on the operation and interplay of social factors, conforms in general to the modern convention. But no analysis of the temporary incapacity for further European conquest which overtook the formidable Turkish war machine and imperial system from the death of Suleiman the Magnificent to the middle of the seventeenth century can entirely neglect the evident decline in the personal quality of the line of Ottoman sultans.

Suleiman's immediate successor, Selim II, 'the Sot', provides an early illustration of a growing tendency for sultans to become prisoners of the harem or impresarios of a bizarre troupe of court favourites. Seventeenth-century sultans rarely went on campaign; when they did, it was usually in an ornamental capacity. Suleiman and his great predecessors never shrank from violence; but the violence practised by the rulers who succeeded them tended to be self-indulgent and capricious in motivation – the violence of a Nero rather than that of a Caesar. Some seventeenth-century sultans were simple-minded, like Mustapha, who was twice deposed for idiocy, in 1618 and again in 1622, and Ibrahim I (1644–8). Even an effective ruler like Murad IV (1623–40) gives an impression of furious and misdirected energy, uninformed and uncontrolled by considerations of long-term policy. These deficiencies in the personal qualities of the sultans need not, in a more favourable context, have seriously affected the whole character and working of the empire. In Europe the growth of bureaucracy enabled many a state of the seventeenth and eighteenth centuries to survive without serious consequence the worst eccentricities of kings who were madmen or minors. The expansion of Ottoman bureaucracy was parallel with that of the European powers, but with one important difference. The Dutch observer Rycaut wrote: 'If a man considers the contexture of the whole Turkish government, he will find it such a fabric of slavery, that it is a wonder if any amongst them should be born of a free, ingenious spirit.' The central importance of slavery in the Ottoman military and administrative system placed enormous powers and responsibilities of decision-making in the monarch's hands. The strongest Grand Vizier was still a creature of the sultan; even if he arranged the assassination of one incompetent ruler, he was equally at the mercy of the next. To a far greater extent than any contemporary European state the Ottoman empire was dependent for its animation and direction on the presence upon the throne of a ruler capable of exercising – or rationally delegating – control. This requirement was seldom fulfilled during the late sixteenth and the first half of the seventeenth century.

The unconcealed hostility and disapproval underlying Rycaut's verdict should not prevent us from recognizing its essential perceptiveness. Many Ottoman officials of the early seventeenth century were aware that something had gone seriously wrong; none was capable of offering a profound or penetrating analysis of the situation. This was not for want of effort; Murad IV commissioned from a prominent Moslem jurist, Khodji-Beg, a *Rissala* or memorandum on the causes of decline. This is a pathetic document when compared with the searching, tough-minded political literature being produced in contemporary Europe. The *Rissala* consists of little more than a catalogue of superficial symptoms. It is, nevertheless, an important piece of historical evidence. What is significant is the prescription for recovery which Khodji-Beg urges on his master; not reform but regeneration, not innovation but a return to traditional practices in the purity of their original form. The ruling caste of the Ottoman empire was evidently succumbing to a profound conservatism and reluctance to face reality which were far removed from the imperious determination to master events which characterized their sixteenth-century predecessors. Any satisfactory interpretation of seventeenth-century Ottoman history must include some explanation of this change in the psychology of the governing class.

Even the full muster of the Ottoman empire no longer sufficed to win more than trifling successes on the Hungarian frontier. To the east the frontier still lay open, for in Pontic Europe there was no equivalent of the broad belt of fortresses which barred further advance into Hungary. Wide and potentially fertile lands were available to the first intruder capable of establishing a regime

favourable to settlement. But Turkish influence in this region rested on alliance with the Crimean Tartars, whose slave raids had created a desert in much of it. Some Ottoman statesmen and strategists were not content to leave the area north of the Black Sea in this undeveloped condition. In 1569 a Turkish expeditionary force penetrated as far as Astrakhan and began to construct a canal connecting the Don with the Volga. But Russian resistance at Astrakhan, the reluctance of the Crimean Tartars to cooperate with Ottoman troops in an enterprise which, if successful, would have hemmed in the wide-ranging Tartars as never before, and the deserted countryside itself, which made living off the land impracticable, combined to inflict a heavy defeat on the Turks. Of the 30,000 men who sailed from Constantinople in 1569 only 7,000 returned the next year with nothing to show for their efforts. After such a débâcle the enterprise was never resumed.

93 Periods of European relief from Ottoman pressure usually coincided with Turkish campaigns in the east, particularly against Persia. The Ottoman commander (on the right) enters Tiflis, capital of Persia's vassal state of Georgia, in 1578, preceded by a detachment of janissaries

The year 1570 therefore signifies the temporary exhaustion of Ottoman capacity for expansion both in Danubian and in Pontic Europe. The other frontiers of the empire failed to offer any adequate substitute for the European victories by which the Turkish military machine and governing caste had been both tested and sustained. Expansion on these eastern borders did not cease. Naval and military expeditions to the Red Sea asserted Ottoman control over the *Hejaz* in southern Arabia in 1571. Even more impressive, at least on the map, were the Turkish conquests in Georgia and Azerbaijan which resulted from a long war against Persia from 1577 to 1590. But the reality of Ottoman administrative control of these regions was always questionable. Azerbaijan was already Moslem, and the local landowners and tribal chieftains were not superseded; while Georgia remained under its Christian rulers in a condition of suzerainty analogous to that of the principality of Transylvania. New fiefs did not become available for distribution among Ottoman warriors.

Throughout the empire *sipahis* therefore tended to settle down as tenants of particular estates. As a result the flexible Ottoman military system underwent rapid and drastic mutation. Rootless warriors, who lived in the saddle as part of an ever-victorious army and cared little about their offspring and descendants, transformed themselves into lazy landlords inhabiting provincial towns where their tenants brought them the dues on which they lived.

This growing attachment of the *sipahis* to particular locations entailed further complications. A natural desire to pass on property and position to one's sons placed a severe strain on the Ottoman legal principle which stated that properties were to be granted to fighting men only during their lifetime as a means of winter subsistence and a recompense for services rendered. Sons might not be of age when their fathers died. Even in the time of Suleiman the Magnificent this led to difficulties; and in 1530 the sultan issued elaborate regulations prescribing what proportion of a deceased warrior's income should go to his sons not yet of age, with higher percentages assigned to those whose fathers had died in battle than to those whose fathers had died of natural causes. The drive towards hereditary succession among the military élite of the empire gathered

166

strength in subsequent generations, subverting the bureaucratic rationality of the regime which Suleiman inherited and perfected.

This change in ethos among the ruling military class of the Ottoman empire found expression in a decrease in individual recklessness in battle and in administrative flexibility behind the lines. In consequence, the effective power at the personal disposition of the sultan was seriously reduced during the first half of the seventeenth century. Yet the fabric of Ottoman society remained, grand and imposing; and Ottoman culture retained its power of attracting aliens long after 1570. The Ottoman empire did not precisely decay; it merely descended towards the normal level of fiscal and administrative confusion to which the states of western Europe, Moslem India and North Africa had long been accustomed.

As normal confusion and variety set in, Ottoman and Christian rulers began to operate within comparable limitations and according to much the same pattern. In Ottoman as in European society an hereditary landowning class struggled against the discipline imposed by an absolute monarchy served by appointed officials who had no hereditary claim to power. This struggle assumed a particularly dramatic form in Russia, where the period has been traditionally called The Time of Troubles. We may apply the same term to the internal difficulties experienced by the Ottoman empire between 1570 and 1650.

THE OTTOMAN TIME OF TROUBLES: 1570–1650

After 1570 the Turks remained almost continuously at war, but campaigns were now seldom crowned by overwhelming victory and permanent conquest. The effort invested in distant enterprises against Spain and Italy, against the Persians in eastern Anatolia and against the Habsburgs in Hungary tended to lessen as the prospect of any important gain evaporated. Fief holders became increasingly unwilling to accept mobilization for military adventures which promised nothing but hardship and danger. At the same time various practices flourished outside or on the margin of the law which allowed sons to succeed to their father's lands, often without undertaking the obligation of military service.

167

In the same period the royal slave household, the principal agency through which the sultan exercised personal control over both civil and military affairs, also threatened to get out of hand. The imperial finances, like those of individual Turkish warriors, formerly depended on substantial booty income. The decisive superiority of Ottoman over European arms in the first half of the sixteenth century was partly attributable to the immense resources of the sultan, which enabled him to maintain a larger, better-equipped and more firmly disciplined force than any rival. These resources were accumulated by preying upon the borderlands where the imperial field army operated each summer. This was no longer possible when summer operations, so far from enriching, were more likely to impoverish rulers and soldiers who participated in lengthy campaigns against desolate frontier outposts which, even when captured, yielded no booty worth the name.

What could no longer be obtained from the frontier zones of the empire was made good by increased exactions from the subject populations at home. Landlords demanded extra dues and services from the peasants on their estates. Officials of the sultan's slave household demanded extra payments, whether for the performance of the duties of their office or for non-performance of these duties in exchange for bribes. Such practices enabled both *sipahis* and royal officials to live in a more luxurious style than their predecessors had done in the days of rapid territorial expansion and abundant booty income.

The lower ranks of the armed forces, however, enjoyed few such opportunities. With a general inflation of prices, resulting in part from the infiltration of Spanish American silver into the economic systems of the Mediterranean world, their pay became increasingly inadequate. The solution officially adopted was that of allowing the *élite* infantry corps, the janissaries, to work as artisans during their idle time in garrison, supplementing their pay from the sale of manufactured goods. But just as venturesome *sipahis* were beginning to transform themselves into parasitic landlords, so too the common soldiers, once their livelihood came to depend on the sale of artisan products, tended to dissolve into the artisan population of

Constantinople and other garrison towns, and lost much of their traditional discipline and thirst for battle.

When the janissaries took up artisan trades and began to mix freely with the civilian population, it became extremely difficult to prevent the operation of the hereditary principle. Sons of janissaries were at first only admitted to the corps under cover of a legal fiction, for no born Moslem could lawfully be enslaved. Under Selim II (1566–74) a quota was established for admission of janissaries' sons to the muster rolls; and in 1638 Sultan Murad IV finally abolished the traditional method of recruitment to the imperial slave household through child tribute exacted from the villages of the western Balkans. This enactment gave legal recognition to an already accomplished fact. The sons of office holders had for a long time been seeping into the privileged ranks of the royal household; all available posts could be filled without the necessity of recourse to forcible recruitment from remote Balkan villages.

This evolution of Ottoman institutions conspicuously favoured urban populations at the expense of the peasants in the heartlands of the empire. While a majority of the ruling caste was drawn from enslaved village boys, a vestigial sympathy for the peasant populations from which they sprang held townsmen and the landlord class in check. No such charitable sentiments affected the conduct of officials who had grown up in towns and entered the royal slave household through family influence or the purchase of office. These men based their reputation and careers on the practice of extreme ruthlessness in fiscal administration which, if efficiently pursued, permitted them to purchase ever higher office.

The old military virtues remained important, but even competent commanders frequently forfeited their reputations on distant frontiers where victory, though still expected, could no longer easily be obtained. By contrast, a clever, pushing man who stayed close to the seat of power in Constantinople might profit as much from military failure as from success – if he joined the winning faction soon enough or paid the right official sufficient money to purchase a new and more lucrative office. Cynical political expertise flourished in this environment. But the men who rose to the top were the survivors of stern competition; they were normally endowed with unusual energy and intelligence even though trained in a narrow, conservative and morally unscrupulous tradition.

The growing importance of towns in Ottoman society stimulated and was stimulated by an increase in the luxury, level of cultivation and mere numbers of the upper classes. During the sixteenth century *sipahis* who were sons or grandsons of penniless villagers or half-starved tribesmen accepted a spartan existence while on campaign as part of the natural order of things and, in winter quarters, lacked time and opportunity to make more than a superficial acquaintance with the seductions of urbanity. Their descendants, leisured town-dwelling landlords who took to the saddle seldom and reluctantly, provided on the one hand an enlarged market for merchants and craftsmen and on the other demanded more dues and higher rents from the peasants who sustained them. A wide gap thus opened between town and country. Village populations became alienated from the Ottoman establishment. The remarkable rise of brigandage in the seventeenth-century Balkans provides a good index of this development. Young men who in an earlier time might have been drafted into the royal household, to emerge, in some cases, as rulers of the empire, now tended under the pressure of cruel taxation to become bandits, whose occasional attacks upon Ottoman officials or townsmen did not prevent them from living most of the time as parasites upon the Orthodox Christian peasantry.

What happened may be described in another way by saying that a military and administrative hierarchy which had initially nourished itself by plundering the borderlands of the expanding Ottoman state transferred the zone of its predation towards the centre of the empire as the borderlands became exhausted. The extraordinary and contrived Ottoman social system of the fifteenth and sixteenth centuries, having reached the technical limits of expansion, was painfully readjusting to a style of life in which large booty windfalls were no longer available.

The strain imposed upon Ottoman institutions by the cessation of territorial expansion and the decline in booty income produced a long series of disturbances and palace revolutions in Constantinople,

94, 95 The growth of superstition and
religious formalism was both cause
and consequence of Ottoman decline.
The amulet (above), 'the hand of
Fatima' (daughter of the Prophet),
comes from Sarajevo, late sixteenth or
early seventeenth century. Right,
Sultan Mohammed III

usually inspired by the janissaries and other household troops or by
the students and officials of the religious establishments of the city.
In 1589 the janissaries mutinied when their pay was delivered in
debased coinage and forced the dismissal of the Grand Vizier and
other high officials. This was the first time that common soldiers
intervened successfully in high politics; but the experience soon
became commonplace. In 1622 and again in 1648 janissary mutineers
deposed and executed the sultan.

Despite these and many less drastic outbursts, the Ottoman
military and administrative system remained capable of sporadic
recovery. In 1596, for example, Sultan Mohammed III mobilized
the whole resources of the empire for a campaign against the Austrian Habsburgs which accumulated plunder on something like the
traditional scale. A more extended revival came during the reign of
Sultan Murad IV (1623–40). A firm adherent of the principle that
'rien n'avance les choses comme les exécutions', Murad savagely
punished administrative corruption and military incompetence. He
also planned far-reaching military reforms aimed at producing a

171

smaller but well-paid and fully professional army. But his early death cancelled all his reforms with the exception of the suspension of Balkan child tribute, which happened to coincide with the self-interest of the Ottoman ruling class. Under normal conditions, however, when central authority was not exercised by a ruthless and energetic sultan or Grand Vizier, the consolidation of vested interests continued. Any attempt to galvanize the imperial system into effective military action ran into increasing opposition and demanded progressively greater expenditure of administrative effort.

Ottoman rulers were in fact trapped in a difficult dilemma. Reform implied innovation; but threatened vested interests invariably insisted that what was necessary to keep the empire great was not innovation, but a faithful conformity with precedent. Janissary privileges should not be infringed and the traditional tactics and equipment of Turkish armies must remain unaltered. European developments in military technology were irrelevant. The will of Allah, which had endorsed ancient custom by granting the Ottomans overwhelming successes in the sixteenth century, could not change. Had these triumphs been less spectacular and the past a less persuasive model of successful action, thorough-going reforms of the sort which were accomplished by Ivan the Terrible and later Peter the Great in Russia might have been more easily implemented. The Russians, being without a great imperial past, could afford to model themselves upon foreigners; the Turks, on the other hand, found it impossible to liberate themselves from Ottoman traditions.

One corollary of this deeply conservative outlook was that the curtailment of autocratic power never proceeded so far in the Ottoman empire as in European states. The instruments of absolutism were always latent in Turkish society, even when weaklings or children occupied the throne. Ruthless and able men continued to staff the Ottoman administration, although they ceased to aim primarily at matters of public concern, concentrating instead on the narrow but no less engrossing game of self-aggrandizement, self-enrichment and defence against rivals. Yet the presence of a strong-willed and intelligent ruler at the head of such a hierarchy could, within a relatively short space of time, polarize the ranks of the bureaucracy like the molecules of a magnet, making them an obedient instrument of a single sovereign will. This, as we shall see, was the achievement of the Grand Viziers, Mohammed and Ahmed Kuprülü. But the overpowering traditionalism of Ottoman society which permitted such revivals also limited the effective action of the restored bureaucratic instrument to traditional means and goals.

The same conservative cast of mind interfered with the free working of hereditary privilege. Even when this had become widespread in practice, dominating the system of landholding and operating throughout many branches of government, it was still felt to be fundamentally wrong, a usurpation which might rightfully be overridden by a strong ruler and his appointed agents.

Thus, however murderous the interplay of mob politics and rival factions in Constantinople, the Ottoman Time of Troubles was comparatively superficial, leading to no lasting or fundamental alteration in the balance of social forces and eliciting no significant departure from established ideas and ideals of life and government.

RENEWED OTTOMAN ADVANCE: 1650–83

Ottoman conquests of the fifteenth and sixteenth centuries conjured into existence on the fringes of the empire in eastern and Pontic Europe a chain of client states, Transylvania, Moldavia, Wallachia and the Tartar khanates around the Black Sea and the Sea of Azov, which, though never formally conquered or colonized, were subject to an effective tributary relationship. One consequence of the internal difficulties experienced by the Ottoman empire during the first half of the seventeenth century was a series of attempts by a crop of colourful military adventurers to establish in these regions despotic regimes which were at once independent of Ottoman control and resistant to the blandishments of the land-hungry Habsburgs.

The comparative success which initially attended the exertions and intrigues of these princelings was abruptly reversed during the middle years of the century. Campaigns during the 1640s restored Ottoman control over the khans of the Crimea and the Sea of Azov. By the Treaty of Westphalia in 1648 the European powers had recognized and guaranteed the independence of Transylvania; but in 1658 a Turkish army arrived to reassert Ottoman suzerainty. In the same period the operations of Turkish agents and Greek financiers who were Ottoman subjects, together with the gravitational pull exercised upon Rumanian agriculture by the incessant demands of the metropolitan food market in Constantinople, returned Moldavia and Wallachia to the Ottoman orbit. This was clear evidence that the Turkish empire was, if only temporarily, surmounting its internal difficulties and renewing its capacities for conquest and absorption.

The earliest sign of a reviving appetite for wars of aggression against Europeans came in the Mediterranean in 1645, when the Ottomans invaded Crete, one of the most jealously guarded remaining outposts of the republic of Venice. Turkish troops quickly cleared the Venetians from the island, but their failure to take the citadel of Candia entangled both sides in a long and painful siege war. The unimpressive military performance of the Ottoman forces in the early stages of the Cretan campaign has diverted the attention of most historians from one incidental development of far-reaching importance. Resistance was offered only by the Venetian garrison, which was supplied and reinforced from the mother-city. The Greek islanders at first welcomed the Turks as liberators from the oppressive rule of Roman Catholic Italians; then, in succeeding years, they began to undergo conversion to Islam in substantial numbers.

This was a startling reversal of Ottoman experience during the sixteenth century. With the exception of the forcible conversion of Balkan slave boys recruited to staff the imperial household, the Ottomans had shown little interest during the reign of Suleiman the Magnificent and his immediate successors in spreading their religion among the conquered peoples of eastern Europe. The rigid Sunnite orthodoxy which was espoused by the government, while enjoining toleration of Christianity upon true believers, emphasized the difference between Moslem belief and that of other religions; and the proscription of fringe groups of dervish heterodoxy suppressed one of the means by which adherents of other faiths had traditionally been coaxed into acceptance of Islam.

All ecclesiastical systems experience rhythmic alternations of puritanical orthodoxy with eclectic, heterodox attitudes. The inevitable reaction from the rigorous and narrowly defined version of Islam imposed by Suleiman was quickened by a series of wars against Persia during the first half of the seventeenth century, which, beneath the ebb and flow of formal military hostilities, exposed the eastern frontier of the Ottoman empire to an influx of heretical Shi'a influences. The janissaries had always maintained close links with the dervish order of the Bektashi; and frequent janissary interventions in palace politics introduced radical speculative tendencies into the highest circles of imperial administration. What Islam as practised in the Ottoman empire during the seventeenth century lost in doctrinal rigour it gained in attractive power and capacity for making converts.

The Cretan conversions suggested that certain remote and poverty-stricken communities among the subject Christian peoples of the empire might respond to the opportunities inherent in this changed situation, seeking to improve their prospects of employment in government service by crossing in large numbers from Christianity to Islam. This possibility was confirmed as mass conversion among Albanian and Montenegrin mountaineers and among the Bulgars of the Rhodope mountains gathered momentum throughout the remainder of the century.

Albanian converts were destined to play a crucial role in the revival of the Ottoman empire. Avenues of advancement still lay open in the Ottoman army and administration to thrusting and capable careerists of humble peasant origin. Albanians swarmed down from their mountains in the middle years of the seventeenth century to undertake functions which had been fulfilled during the sixteenth century by Bosnian and Serbian slaves. The martial skills and attitudes which they brought with them from their homelands alone sufficed, when introduced at a thousand points into the army and administration, to impart a renewed aggressive character to Ottoman policy. The legacy of tribal custom made them selfless and dedicated royal servants of a kind which had now grown rare in the Turkish empire. To the Albanian mountaineers the most binding agreement was the *besa* or oath of friendship, originally a device for the compounding of the blood feuds which bedevilled their society. The *besa* acquired a new significance for those Albanians who entered the service of the sultan. They considered the forms of agreement which were incidental to taking service in the royal household as equivalent to their traditional oath of solidarity and friendship. Albanian migrants to the cities of the Ottoman empire thus transferred to their employers the fierce devotion reserved in their homeland for sworn friends and comrades-in-arms, and they could be relied upon to identify their own interests with those of their master and to honour their oath of obedience under pressures which would have alienated any other ethnic group in the Ottoman empire.

Not only did the Cretan war provide a forecast of this future; it also projected to the direction of Ottoman affairs a dynasty of Grand Viziers, the Kuprülü family, which was capable of setting the empire upon a renewed career of conquest. A janissary mutiny, expressive of widespread dissatisfaction with the conduct of the war, deposed and executed Sultan Ibrahim in 1648. In 1656 further popular disturbances in Constantinople followed a Venetian naval victory in the Dardanelles. An old and respected Ottoman official who began his career as a scullion in the imperial kitchens, Mohammed Kuprülü, was called from retirement to take office as Grand Vizier. Kuprülü accepted only upon condition that his power should be absolute and unchallenged. The emphatic policy which he followed during the five years before his death in 1661 transformed the situation. He drove the Venetians from the strategic islands of Lemnos and Tenedos. In 1658 he launched a series of military expeditions which installed obedient puppet princes on the thrones of Transylvania, Moldavia and Wallachia. At home ferocious measures were taken to improve the quality of administration and restore discipline amongst the household troops.

Mohammed Kuprülü was succeeded as Grand Vizier by his son Ahmed, who governed until 1676. Inheriting a military organization which his father had returned to something approaching its sixteenth-century level of efficiency, Ahmed celebrated his assumption of

96 The outcry in Constantinople following a Venetian victory in the Dardanelles (above) brought the able and energetic Kuprülü family to the direction of Ottoman affairs in 1656

office by preparing the now traditional campaign against the Habsburgs in Hungary, Moravia and Silesia. The Ottomans put an army of over 200,000 men into the field in 1663; but this attack was essentially a *razzia*, a great – and successful – plunder operation rather than a campaign of territorial conquest. When they resumed hostilities in the following year, the Ottomans encountered resolute and well-organized resistance. The Imperialist army had been stiffened by a large contingent of French troops whose military techniques were the most advanced of the period, and entrusted to

177

the command of a brilliant Italian general, Raimondo Montecuccoli; and at the Battle of St Gothard the Turks sustained a crushing defeat. Frustrated in war, Ahmed Kuprülü fell back on the arts of diplomacy; although the terms of the truce of Vasvar (1664) obliged the Ottomans to surrender parts of Turkish Hungary to the Habsburgs, they obtained in recompense the concession of certain frontier fortresses which they had captured from the Austrians during the campaign of 1663.

It was nevertheless clear that the Habsburgs now disposed of field forces whose well-drilled and competently commanded infantry and artillery units were capable in normal circumstances of inflicting an intolerable casualty rate on advancing Ottoman armies. Ahmed Kuprülü therefore decided to probe for weaker spots in the European system of defences. He pursued the Cretan war with such vigour that Candia capitulated and the Venetians abandoned the island in

97 Plan of the battle of St Gothard, 1664. In an eight-hour engagement the Turkish army was torn to pieces by the concentrated fire-power of an Austrian army defending the south bank of the river Raab

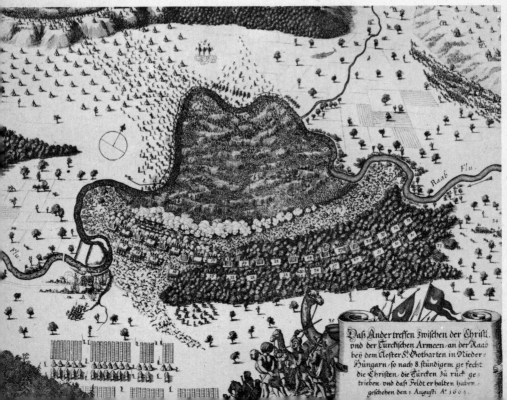

98, 99 John III Sobieski, king of Poland (1629–96), and Raimondo Montecuccoli, the victor of St Gothard

1669. This success freed Turkish forces for new ventures in the north. The Ukraine offered tempting possibilities; the region was disputed between Russia and Poland, with the native Cossack communities attempting to win independence from both. A series of ruthlessly destructive Ottoman expeditions into the Polish Ukraine during the 1670s enabled Ahmed Kuprülü to crown his career by dictating the Treaty of Zuravno to John Sobieski, king of Poland, in 1676. The Poles abandoned all territorial claims in the region; a large Ukrainian province (Podolia) was taken under direct Ottoman administration; and a second area, the homeland of the Zaporozhian Cossacks on the west bank of the Dnieper, was declared subject to Turkish suzerainty.

The Kuprülü family was Albanian by origin; and the successes of the first two Kuprülü Grand Viziers were probably connected with the links which were being forged by mass conversion during the second half of the seventeenth century between the Ottoman government and the Albanian mountain tribes. These recruits infused a new energy and enthusiasm into both the army and the bureaucracy. In partial, but still effective fashion, the old tradition of recruitment from below into the ruling caste persisted or revived; by this means some of the energy of Ottoman administration, once so remarkable, survived the corruption and vested interests introduced into the management of the empire during the seventeenth century by the enhanced power of urban and landowning groups. Yet the Kuprülü revival was to prove more spectacular than solid. Conversions were restricted to the barren mountain areas of Albania, Crete and southern Bulgaria. The mass population of the Balkans, especially the plainsmen and the ploughing peasants, remained aloof from and untouched by Islam in the seventeenth century as in the sixteenth. The flow of migration from the mountains reinvigorated the governing classes of the empire but was insufficient to alter the terms or affect the outcome of the profound and debilitating social crisis which underlay the Ottoman Times of Troubles.

Even the dramatic successes achieved by Ahmed Kuprülü in the Ukraine during the early 1670s lacked the permanence and stability of the great Balkan conquests of the Turks in the sixteenth century. Russian pressure forced the Ottomans to disgorge some of their gains in 1681; and in any case marauding Ottoman armies had created such a desert in the region that its potentialities as a reservoir of manpower, tribute and food supply were blighted for generations.

Ahmed Kuprülü was succeeded as Grand Vizier by his brother-in-law, Kara Mustapha, a self-regarding visionary with far less understanding than the Kuprülüs of the necessity of relating ambitions to resources. Oblivious of the sharp lessons in tactics and military techniques administered by the Austrians during the early 1660s, he abandoned the policy of expansion into the Ukraine in favour of a resumption of hostilities in central Europe against the Habsburgs. To do him justice, the moment seemed opportune. The persistent efforts of the Austrian Habsburgs after 1648 to subject the turbulent Magyar nobility of Hungary to more effective bureaucratic control from Vienna, to promote the spread of the Counter-Reformation throughout their dominions and to plant strong garrisons in Hungary against the Turks provoked growing unrest among many of the local magnates. The Hungarian dissidents looked at first to France for supplies and diplomatic support; but French assistance fell away after the conclusion of the Peace of Nimwegen between France and Austria in 1678. Kara Mustapha in Constantinople quickly came forward with offers to replace Louis XIV as the patron of Magyar resistance to Habsburg centralization. He found a willing collaborator, and the mutinous Hungarian magnates an athletic if intellectually limited leader, in Imre Tökölli, a young nobleman whose grandfather had been executed for plotting rebellion against the Habsburgs in 1671. In many respects Tökölli's career as a representative of Hungarian 'magnate patriotism', allying with the Ottoman empire in order to frustrate the progress of Austrian bureaucratization, recalls that of John Zapolyai during the sixteenth century.

Kara Mustapha's dream of overwhelming victory at the expense of the Habsburgs necessitated a delay of several years after his appointment to office while a huge Ottoman army was being assembled and trained for the enterprise. The Habsburgs took typically astute advantage of this breathing space to modify the inflexibility of their Hungarian policy. When in 1681 he reinstated the ancient constitution of the kingdom, the Emperor Leopold I deprived Imre Tökölli of support from those members of the Magyar nobility who had no wish to evade the commands of the emperor in Vienna only to fall into the clutches of the sultan in Constantinople.

100 Imre Tökölli

101 Kara Mustapha

In the spring of 1683 Kara Mustapha unleashed his gigantic and polyglot army, drawn from all the vassal provinces and client states of the Ottoman empire along the Danube. Habsburg field forces in Hungary were rolled back by weight of numbers; overwhelmed at Petronell, they retreated into Vienna; and in July the Turks arrived to undertake their second historic siege of the city. Europe echoed with flesh-creeping predictions of the outcome should Vienna fall. Even the sour Louis XIV, the most single-minded practitioner of 'raison d'état', was persuaded – at the price of important diplomatic concessions – to agree to refrain for the duration of the crisis from attacking the western frontiers of the Holy Roman Empire.

After a sixty-day siege, Vienna was delivered by a Polish and Imperialist army under the competent command of the King of Poland, John Sobieski. The Ottoman army, outmanœuvred and battered into retreat, was preserved from annihilation only by divisions which broke out among its European adversaries immediately the tide was turned. John Sobieski wrote: 'Here we are on the Danube, like the Israelites on the Euphrates, lamenting the loss of our horses and the ingratitude of those whom we have saved.' Kara Mustapha himself had risked too much and failed too disastrously; he was executed by order of the sultan. His overthrow marks the point at which the military and political initiative in eastern Europe passed permanently from the hands of the Ottomans.

102 The price of failure: the execution of Kara Mustapha

The balance of military power, which favoured the Turks during the reign of Suleiman the Magnificent and left Ottomans and Europeans in a situation of strategic deadlock from 1570 to the late seventeenth century, now inclined definitively in favour of the Austrians and their allies. The exertions of a capable and energetic Grand Vizier could still revive the Ottoman administrative and military system, as was shown during his brief tenure of office (1689–91) by Mustapha Zadé, son of Mohammed Kuprülü; but a prolonged series of military defeats and territorial losses showed that the old aggressive impulse was exhausted. The fact that the Turks surrendered only outlying provinces of their European empire during the remaining years of the seventeenth century is more attributable to quarrels and divisions among the European powers than to their own capacity for continued resistance.

Mobilization of an army to replace that which fell to pieces before Vienna in 1683 occupied the Ottoman government for several years. Habsburg commanders were quick to exploit the situation. In 1684 they swept Imre Tökölli and his remaining supporters from the fortress towns of Turkish Hungary, and in 1686 they stormed the provincial capital and strategic base of Buda. Most of the old kingdom of Hungary was now liberated from Moslem occupation. In 1687 the Turks put their restored army into the field, meeting the Austrians at Mohacs, the same battlefield on which Suleiman the Magnificent had shattered the forces of the Hungarian king and his magnates in 1526. This time victory went to the Christians, who followed up their success by thrusting into Moldavia, Wallachia and Croatia, and obliging Transylvania to renounce Ottoman suzerainty. While the Turks were under heavy pressure in Hungary, the Venetians struck in south-eastern Europe, invading the Morea, capturing Athens and Corinth and driving the Ottomans from most of Dalmatia between 1686 and 1688. During 1688 the Habsburgs remorselessly exploited their victory at Mohacs, capturing the city and fortress of Belgrade, the key to the middle Danube, and pushing their scouting columns as far as Vidin, below the Iron Gates in Bulgaria, and Niš in southern Serbia.

The enforced withdrawal of Austrian troops from the Danubian theatre of operations to combat the aggressions of Louis XIV of France in the Palatinate (1688) afforded the Turks a breathing space which was well used by Mustapha Zadé. In 1690 he recaptured Niš and Belgrade and reasserted Ottoman influence in Transylvania, where Imre Tökölli was installed as prince. But these were mere delaying operations; in 1697 the Austrian government was able to withdraw troops from Italy for further employment in eastern Europe. In that year a brilliant new Habsburg commander, Prince Eugene of Savoy, assembled a mobile, experienced and well-equipped Austrian force which inflicted an overwhelming defeat on the Ottoman army at Zenta on the river Theiss in Transylvania.

Revolts in Arabia and Mesopotamia, the hardships of sustaining a major war effort for so many years and the advice of Dutch and English ambassadors all urged upon the Ottoman government the necessity of initiating peace negotiations. Turkish pride resented loss of territory and open admission of a major defeat at Christian hands; yet the same pride made the only rational alternative even less welcome. Only if Turkish armies had been prepared to abandon their traditions and systematically imitate European military techniques could the Ottoman government hope for victory. But this would have offended Turkish *amour propre* even more than the signature of a disgraceful peace treaty. Having lost four successive armies in the field, the Ottomans were ready to yield territory in order to escape the still more painful surrender of institutional and cultural autonomy.

By the treaty signed at Karlowitz in January 1699, the Turks conceded most of Hungary, including Transylvania, to Austria; returned Podolia to Poland; confirmed the right of the Russians to occupation of the port of Azov; and made over most of Dalmatia, the Morea and the Aegean islands to Venice.

MILITARY AND ECONOMIC PROBLEMS

European commentators of the sixteenth century were united in their praise of Ottoman military organization. In the course of the late seventeenth-century wars outlined above, that organization was

103, 104 Title-page of the Treaty of Ḳarlowitz, 1699. Right, Prince Eugene of Savoy

shown to be outmoded and inefficient. The Turks had failed to keep pace with the times. The governing caste of the Ottoman empire looked with disfavour on any tampering with traditional military techniques and practices. Popular riots and *coups d'état*, they argued, rationalizing the experience of The Time of Troubles, would inevitably result from such a policy; and no Peter the Great came to the Ottoman throne who was willing to confront these dangers in order to use the autocratic powers of his office for revolutionary purposes. No Grand Vizier could work such a revolution, for he was always vulnerable to court intrigues. The rigorous conservatism inculcated by Moslem education, which taught that success and failure, in war as in peace, depended upon Allah's inscrutable will and not upon instruments shaped by the hands of men, also made any programme of radical change seem both irrelevant and impious.

185

The hard and prolonged experience of the Thirty Years War familiarized Germany and central Europe with sophisticated military techniques which were first developed in France and Italy. Profound changes in military organization were beginning to reward bureaucratized armies with victory and to condemn other forms of military effort to defeat. Well-trained professional infantry proved capable of sustaining even the most furious cavalry charge; when supported by artillery, they could massacre their attackers. The more vigorous the assault, the more disastrous the outcome for the old-fashioned cavalry armies of the type which formerly dominated the battlefields of eastern Europe.

The Ottomans were among the earliest powers to grasp the importance of artillery, and probably used cannon at the first Battle of Kossovo in 1389; but here, as in other spheres, they remained prisoners of their origins. While operating as a cavalry horde, the Turks were irresistible in open country but experienced serious difficulties in reducing fortified towns. They therefore welcomed and developed artillery primarily as a siege arm, specializing in the construction of cannon of enormous weight and bore. This emphasis on the production of siege guns, too heavy for use in a war of movement, persisted throughout the seventeenth century, as also did the practice of casting guns only in brass – though this was probably due to the fact that the Ottoman empire contained few and poor deposits of iron, but rich copper mines in Anatolia. During the same period, with the Swedes leading the way, European progress in the manufacture of highly mobile field artillery was rapid and substantial. A serious gap in artillery technology thus opened between Europeans and Turks, the significance of which was realized and stressed by Raimondo Montecuccoli, the victor of St Gothard:

this enormous artillery produces great damage when it hits, but it is awkward to move and it requires too much time to reload and site. Furthermore, it consumes a great amount of powder, besides cracking and breaking the wheels and the carriages and even the ramparts on which it is placed . . . our artillery is more handy to move and more efficient and here resides our advantage over the cannon of the Turks.

105 Fifteenth-century Turkish cannon. This brass siege gun weighs over 18 tons and has a 25-inch calibre

An efficient artillery was an invaluable asset; but in the late seventeenth century the really decisive factor in war was a large army of thoroughly trained and well-equipped infantry regiments. The provision of such a force was an enormously expensive undertaking – which probably explains the fact that in eastern Europe the large bureaucratic empires which alone could contemplate such expenditure re-established control over those interstitial principalities which had prospered and achieved a degree of autonomy and independence during the first half of the seventeenth century, when each of the great powers was experiencing severe internal difficulties. The central problem confronting all eastern European governments with pretensions to great power status was that of fashioning from available social and economic resources an effective war machine on the new pattern. Local peculiarities of religion, culture or social structure might influence the means adopted or the measure of success which was achieved; but the essential goal remained the same, whether for Greek Orthodox Romanovs in Russia, Catholic Habsburgs in Austria or Ottoman sultans in Moslem Turkey.

During the fifteenth and sixteenth centuries the Ottomans relied on two devices to provide the economic and financial infrastructure of their military establishment: the *timar* system and the acquisition of plunder. In spite of widespread and persistent pressure from vested interests which favoured the hereditary principle, the uninheritable fief assigned to the Moslem cavalryman during his lifetime or for his period of active service survived throughout the seventeenth century in some backward areas of the Ottoman empire where subsistence agriculture continued to support fighting men by bringing them back to the land every winter to rest and re-equip. Ottoman armies of the Kuprülü period included large contingents of cavalrymen who wintered in provincial towns and lived on the income of landed estates as their predecessors had done since the days of Suleiman the Magnificent. But such troops were outmoded by the new developments in military organization and technology. Even the reformist Kuprülüs made no serious effort to restore the feudal cavalry by eliminating the innumerable irregularities in the Ottoman landholding system which had arisen with the passage of time.

Plunder, as we have seen, was no longer available in sufficiently large quantities or regular instalments to sustain the laborious enterprise of recruiting, training, paying, feeding and equipping a large army of professional infantry. Seventeenth-century Ottoman rulers, in common with their counterparts in Moscow, Cracow and Vienna, had no choice but to replace plunder by regular taxes as their essential source of supply. Taxes could only be obtained by bureaucratic operations, backed by armed force, against townsmen, peasants and (very occasionally) territorial aristocrats, while the armed forces necessary to back up the bureaucrats were sustained in turn by the taxes which the bureaucrats collected. This circularity could only function vigorously when its supervisors were able to rely upon the availability of money to be taxed and of goods – guns, powder, uniforms, food and an infinity of other items from knapsacks to field marshals' batons – to be bought for the army.

The first of these two necessary conditions was fulfilled in eastern Europe – including the Ottoman dominions – without much deliberate official action, in consequence of the spread of a money economy and the expanding role of commercial agriculture. These developments were the fruits of collaboration between merchants – in Turkish Europe generally Greeks, Jews, Armenians and Serbs, with Greeks predominating in the seventeenth century – and enterprising landlords or local officials, and dated back to the Middle Ages in geographically fortunate and accessible regions. Rural surpluses of meat and grain were transported over comparatively long distances to urban markets, above all to Constantinople, where they sustained the military establishment of the Ottoman empire. Landlocked regions like Transylvania and Hungary lagged behind because of difficulties in bringing their produce to market; but commercial agriculture spread rapidly and continuously during the seventeenth century in most of the plain and riverine lands of eastern Europe. More concentrated and flexible power resulted from the operation of the commercial process; money income, always insufficient to satisfy the growing needs of the state, but for that very reason constantly being enlarged by a steady inflation of tax demands, bribe rates and protection fees, could be turned this way or that, used to build a mosque, to stage a public festival – or to equip a standing army.

106, 107 An Armenian and a Jewish merchant. The economy of the Ottoman empire, no less than its military and administrative system, depended on participation non-Turkish peoples

Thus far the Ottoman government was at least as well placed as any of its eastern European rivals to construct a new-style military system. And the immense forces which Ahmed Kuprülü and Kara Mustapha led into Hungary, though they included contingents of light cavalry proportionately much larger than those which served in contemporary European armies, were indeed mainly composed of professional infantry drawn from the urban populations of Egypt, Greece and the Balkans, and from the rural regions of Anatolia.

What was absent from Turkish practice was coherence and regularity in the financial and banking operations which underlay and sustained this military system. A wide gulf existed in Turkish society between the arts of government and those of commerce. The Turks consigned the capitalist, commercial operation of their empire to subject peoples of a despised religion with a way of life consciously alien from and implicitly opposed to the violence and sensuality affected by the Moslem ruling caste.

Yet the fiscal web spun by Greek, Jewish and Armenian financiers round Ottoman warriors and administrators was straitening despite its gossamer. Only through the operation of a complex financial machine could Constantinople be fed; only through its functioning could Turkish armies be supplied and equipped. But the fact that the ruling groups quite failed to understand how the system operated, tending to believe that in a pinch the threat or application of violence could always be trusted to uncover the necessary cash, exposed the financial structure of the empire to sporadic and cumulatively very damaging crises. The fundamental weakness of seventeenth-century Ottoman society lay in the complete failure of mutual understanding between the governing class on the one hand and the commercial and financial interests on the other, especially when measured against the societies of western Europe, where government and capital, force and money, entered into a more equable alliance, based on shared values and goals which were almost totally lacking in Turkey.

The efficient organization of army supplies, the second necessary condition of military success in the late seventeenth century, was also generally mismanaged by the Ottomans. In part this resulted from their persistent refusal to abandon practices which had enjoyed success in earlier, less complicated times. The systematic rape of the frontier areas enabled sixteenth-century Ottoman forces to live adequately off the land. This was no longer a possibility for seventeenth-century armies, which were often three or four times as large and operating in the depopulated countryside of the Polish Ukraine or the desolate no-man's-land in Hungary. Yet the Ottoman government took no steps to improve or modernize the commissariat. Organization of the supply of weapons and materials for the use of specialist corps such as miners or military engineers was equally casual and negligent. The Habsburgs, with the technical and artisan resources of Germany, Italy and Bohemia at their disposal, were well placed to procure the elaborate and constantly changing equipment required for effective warfare. The artisan force of Constantinople was skilled and numerous, but hidebound and suspicious of innovation. The presence of a powerful and exclusive gild system in Turkish society tended to discourage enterprise and invention. Most gilds were closely affiliated with the janissary companies, whose jealous determination to preserve their traditional military techniques led them to reject all suggestions for improvements in military technology which originated among the artisan groups. Seventeenth-century Ottoman armies were therefore condemned to the use of second-rate and unstandardized matériel.

The Battle of St Gothard in 1664 demonstrated the superiority of a well-trained Habsburg army over any that the Turks, with their relatively haphazard and antiquated financial and supply system, could put into the field. The lapse of some twenty years before this superiority was translated into a continuous sequence of regulated victories was probably due to defects in the Habsburg high command, whose performance was adversely affected by a cumbersome plurality of authority. This was remedied during the campaign of 1683, when Austria's confederates withdrew in such rapid succession from the army which was pursuing the retreating Turks from Vienna that the Habsburgs, finding themselves with a major war on their hands and only their own troops with which to fight it, reformed the high command so that it was more unified and coherent. Once this was so, nothing could save the Ottomans from being driven south of the Danube and east of the Carpathians.

THE HUNGARIAN PROBLEM

Ottoman inroads and occupation left deep and permanent marks on the societies of eastern Europe. Even in retreat the Turks remained capable of sustaining pressures and launching occasional counter-attacks which exercised a shaping influence on the history of European territories which were now outside their direct control. This is well illustrated by developments in Hungary in the 1690s.

When the Ottoman empire began to show signs of revival during the mid-seventeenth century, the Habsburgs took the precaution of establishing a special military administration along the disputed southern border of the Austrian portion of the Hungarian kingdom. Local arrangements were modelled on the much older Croatian *Militärgrenzen*; but administrative control was now lodged in Vienna and not with semi-independent provincial diets as was the case in Croatia. Serbian and Croatian soldier-settlers were planted in these lands, organized into regiments and exempted from ordinary taxation. Affiliated to these settlements a numerous Serbian community, intensely loyal to the Habsburgs, took shape in southern Hungary, where it enjoyed special autonomy under the administration of Orthodox bishops and the Serbian patriarch. Austrian campaigns against the Ottomans during the 1680s carried the front line of hostilities far to the south and east of these one-time frontier colonies; but when in 1690–1 Vienna was forced to withdraw troops from eastern Europe for service against French aggression in the west, the Turks counter-attacked in force and the returning tides of battle inundated the Serbian settlements. The Serbian patriarch presided over a mass exodus of refugees, trekking north from his see at Pécs to Karlowitz with over 100,000 men, women and children in his train. At first this migration was considered as temporary, pending an Austrian military riposte. But continuing distractions in western Europe delayed an Austrian counter-attack for years, and the Serbs settled down north of the Danube under a privileged and semi-autonomous administrative system. The

192

existence of these special regimes on Hungarian soil was particularly distasteful to the Magyar nobility, for communities of free peasants under arms provided a counter-weight to the military predominance of the magnates in the kingdom and a dangerous example to the serfs upon whose labour their income depended.

The sullen and suspicious disposition of the Hungarian nobility which was revealed by this episode was itself intimately connected with Ottoman activities. One distinctive feature of Turkish military practice which suffered no decline from the sixteenth to the seventeenth century was its extreme destructiveness; 'the greatest terrour of the World' was how a matter-of-fact Elizabethan Englishman, Richard Knolles, described the progress of an Ottoman army in *The Generall Historie of the Turkes* (1603). Except when on slaving expeditions, the Turks seldom burdened themselves with prisoners; and their lavish use of *akinjis*, unpaid Tartar light horsemen serving for the reward of plunder and captives in scouting and raiding parties, extended the zone of devastation for many miles in every direction around an army's line of march. In 1683, for example, Kara

108 Title-page of Richard Knolles'
Generall Historie of the Turkes
(1603)

193

Mustapha's advance guards were at the gates of Vienna a week before the arrival of the Grand Vizier with the main forces. The bitter experience of defeat and retreat did nothing to modify the single-minded savagery with which Ottoman armies laid waste the countryside through which they passed. Southern Hungary, which was still affected by the destruction and depopulation caused by the inroads of Suleiman the Magnificent, again suffered terribly at the hands of the Turks during the campaigns of the 1680s and 1690s. This was the unpromising landscape of swamps, sand-dunes and sparsely populated prairies inherited by the Habsburgs by the Treaty of Karlowitz. Deep-seated economic backwardness was inevitable in these circumstances. Until the mid-eighteenth century, livestock – mainly scrubby cattle which lived out-of-doors in winter and summer – constituted the only important export from the Hungarian plains; agriculture was still for the most part a subsistence operation, and the poverty-stricken serfs consumed very little which was not locally produced. This environment, the appalling legacy of Ottoman victory and of Ottoman retreat, imposed a lasting outlook upon the lesser Hungarian nobility. The great magnates migrated to the *salons* and ballrooms of Vienna, becoming thoroughly Austrian in manners and culture. For the minor nobility no such escape route was available, and they retreated into a boorish and archaic localism which exactly reflected - and was powerless to improve – the backward rural society over which they ruled. Theirs was a world utterly apart from the elegant and artificial culture, synthesizing baroque worldliness with Roman Catholic piety, which the Habsburgs were contriving in Vienna.

Once the tide of Turkish conquest had finally receded south of the Danube no compelling external danger existed to drive the Hungarian nobility into the eagerly protective but extremely constricting Austrian embrace. The formidable problem of assimilating this alienated, yet locally all-powerful group into the social and political structure of a centralized Austrian state was to absorb the energies and attentions of Habsburg rulers and bureaucrats throughout the eighteenth and for most of the nineteenth century. Ottoman victories forced an intractable Hungarian problem upon the Habsburgs during the 1520s; and the campaigns which accompanied the period of Turkish withdrawal and defeat between 1683 and 1699 produced social dislocations and economic regression in the same area which enlarged the dimensions of the problem and nullified any possibility that it would soon be solved.

The Treaty of Karlowitz marked a final, decisive turning point in the military balance between Europe and the Islamic world. Sixteen years previously the Ottomans had shown themselves to be still capable of making a vigorous challenge to the west. After Karlowitz the Turkish empire found itself perpetually on the defensive, seldom able to equal the armed strength of any European power. Serious internal disorders, including frequent usurpation of local authority by insubordinate provincial governors and the rapid extension of brigandage – which was later to merge into nationalist resistance movements – in the European dominions of the empire, contributed to this military weakness. The same period witnessed the paralysis and partial disintegration of the two other great Moslem empires, that of the Moguls in India and that of the Safavids in Persia.

Political disorder in the Moslem heartlands blighted economic prosperity. Changing patterns of trade, in particular an increased demand for European textiles and other factory-made goods, depressed the tradition-bound handicraft industries of Moslem towns. Throughout the eighteenth century Moslem economies were everywhere shrinking under European pressure.

109 Coffee house outside the walls of seventeenth-century Vienna. The coffee habit, introduced to Europe by the Turks, is the most benign of all their legacies

Nothing in the past had prepared the Moslem world for such disasters. Until the end of the seventeenth century the outcome of the long conflict between Islam and Christianity generally tended to favour the Moslem cause. This was expected by followers of Allah, whose Prophet Mohammed declared victory in battle against unbelievers to be clear evidence and assurance of divine favour. The abrupt reversal of the trends of history confronted Moslems with a desperate and insoluble problem. Had Allah deserted them? If so, why? And whatever the shortcomings of the faithful, how was it possible that God should favour Christians?

Political disasters had occurred many times in Ottoman history before 1699; but they had always been transitory. The prevailing reaction to the disasters which began at the end of the seventeenth century was to wait patiently for the storm to blow itself out, while remaining true to the past so far as circumstances allowed.

When the storm refused to oblige, timid and clumsy attempts were made to appropriate those achievements of European civilization which seemed responsible for European success. The most obvious was military technology; and from 1716 Ottoman officials were making sporadic efforts to re-create Turkish armies on European models. But for more than a century the adamant conservatism of the janissaries and the *ulema* made every such project abortive. Changes initiated by a reforming sultan or Grand Vizier were repeatedly undone by popular riots or janissary mutinies. Recurrent rebellion at home and continued disasters in war against European powers distracted the sultans from the effort needed to strengthen their military establishment. No overpowering personality ascended the Ottoman throne to carry through a revolution from above; consequently, reform remained stillborn. The vast majority of Moslems were in a state of catalepsy, unable to cope either intellectually or in practice with the new conditions created by European military and cultural superiority. A blind conservatism, clinging to the crumbling landmarks of a vanishing social order, dominated the Ottoman world until well past the middle of the nineteenth century.

1281	Death of *ghazi* chieftain Ertughrul, founder of Ottoman emirate in north-western Anatolia	1444–90	Creation of powerful Hungarian kingdom by John Hunyadi (d. 1458) and Matthias Corvinus
1326	Ottomans capture Brusa: emir Orkhan assumes title of sultan	1448	Turks defeat Hungarian alliance at second battle of Kossovo
1329	Ottomans capture Nicaea	1451	Turks begin third siege of Constantinople
1331–55	Creation of Serbian empire by Stephan Dušan		
1337	Ottomans capture Nicomedia	1452	Genoese lose Phocaea to the Turks
1345	Ottoman Turks enter Europe as mercenaries in Byzantine pay	1453	Turks capture Constantinople and make it the Ottoman capital
1350	Turks capture Salonika	1456	Ottoman army fails to take Belgrade
1352	Turks defeat Serbians at first battle of Maritza river		
1354	Turks capture Adrianople	1456–62	Genoese lose island colonies in the Aegean to the Turks
1362	Turks conquer Thrace	1463	Turkish conquest of Bosnia
1363	Ottoman sultan recognized in European possessions by Byzantine emperor	1464	Failure of projected crusade of Pope Pius II
1366	Adrianople named as capital of Ottoman state	1469	Union of Spanish kingdoms under Ferdinand and Isabella
1371	Following victory at second battle of Maritza river Turks capture Niš and attack Bulgaria	1470	Venice loses Euboea to Turks
		1475	Turks capture Caffa and other Black Sea ports from Genoese
1389	Turks overthrow Serbian empire at first battle of Kossovo	1479	Ottoman conquest of Albania
1393	Turks overrun Bulgaria	1482	Ottoman conquest of Herzegovina
1396	Turks abandon first siege of Constantinople to defeat Crusade of Nicopolis	1484	Turks establish control over mouths of Danube and Dniester
1402	Turks abandon second siege of Constantinople when Mongols invade Asia Minor	1490–1526	Hungarian aristocracy gain ground at expense of Kings Ladislas (d. 1516) and Lewis
1407	Foundation of Bank of St George at Genoa	1492	Fall of Moorish kingdom of Granada; Columbus discovers the New World
1438	Foundation of janissary corps		
1444	Turks defeat Hungarian alliance at battle of Varna	1494	Portuguese navigators reach India by the Cape route

197

1496	Turks establish control over Montenegro: Venice acquires Cyprus	1541	Suleiman's Hungarian conquests formally incorporated into Ottoman empire; failure of Charles V's expedition against Algiers
1499–1508	Ismail Safavi founds Shi'a empire in Persia and Iraq	1543	Franco-Turkish alliance; successful Turkish campaign in Hungary
1502	Spain adopts policy of forcible conversion of Moslem subjects	1544	Barbarossa raids west coast of Italy
1512–20	Selim I (the Grim) sultan	1547	Ferdinand I recognizes Turkish conquests in Hungary
1514	Ottomans suppress Shi'a rebellion in Anatolia and defeat Persia at battle of Tchaldiran; peasants' revolt in Hungary	1551–65	Exploits of North African corsair admiral Dragut operating from Tripoli
1516	Charles V becomes king of Spain	1554	Joseph Nasi moves from Italy to Constantinople
1516–17	Ottoman conquest of Syria and Egypt	1554–62	Busbecq imperial ambassador at Constantinople
1517	Lutheran revolt in Germany	1555	Peace of Augsburg ends religious war in Germany
1519–58	Charles V Holy Roman Emperor		
1520–66	Suleiman the Magnificent sultan	1556–98	Philip II king of Spain
1521	Suleiman captures Belgrade	1557	Bankruptcy of Spanish crown
1521–2	Ferdinand I given control of Habsburg family lands	1559	Treaty of Cateau-Cambrésis frees Habsburgs from dynastic struggle against France
1522	Turks capture Rhodes from Knights of St John	1560	Spanish military and naval disaster at Djerba; death of Andrea Doria
1526	Turkish victory at first battle of Mohacs and fall of kingdom of Hungary	1564–5	Peasant risings against Turks in Macedonia
1526–64	Ferdinand I rules as king of Austria and Habsburg Hungary (Holy Roman Emperor from 1558)	1565	Unsuccessful Turkish siege of Malta
1528	Andrea Doria becomes admiral of Spain and effective ruler of Genoa	1566	Futile Turkish campaign in Hungary; Turks drive Genoese from Chios; Sultan Selim II names Joseph Nasi Duke of Naxos
1529	First unsuccessful Turkish siege of Vienna; Martin Luther preaches crusade against Turks	1568–70	Morisco rebellion in Spain
1534–46	Algerian corsair Khaireddin Barbarossa admiral of Turkish fleet and leader of war party at Constantinople	1569–70	Failure of Turkish expedition to Astrakhan
1535	Expedition led by Charles V recaptures Tunis	1570	Ottomans drive Venetians from Cyprus
1537	Ottoman naval forces attack southern Italy and Corfu	1571	Turkish defeat in naval battle of Lepanto; risings against Ottoman rule in Greece and the Aegean islands
1538	Indecisive naval battle of Prevesa; Suleiman assumes title of caliph		

1573	Withdrawal of Venice from alliance against Turks; English merchants become active in Mediterranean; peasants' revolt against Habsburgs in Croatia and Slovenia	1638	Sultan Murad IV abolishes recruitment into Ottoman slave household from Balkan child tribute
1574	Turks capture Tunis	1639	Lasting peace concluded between Ottoman and Persian empires
1575	Second bankruptcy of Spanish crown	1645	Turks invade Crete
1577	Turks open peace negotiations with Spain	1648	Janissary mutiny deposes and executes Sultan Ibrahim I
1577–90	War between Ottoman and Persian empires	1656–61	Mohammed Kuprülü Grand Vizier
1580	Spanish annexation of Portugal	1658	Ottoman empire strengthens political control over Transylvania, Moldavia and Wallachia
1581	Truce between Ottoman empire and Spain	1661–76	Ahmed Kuprülü Grand Vizier
1584	Renewal of truce between Ottoman empire and Spain	1664	Turks defeated at battle of St Gothard
1585	Spain declares war on England	1669	Venice surrenders Crete to the Turks
1587	Renewal of truce between Ottoman empire and Spain	1676	Treaty of Zuravno recognizes territorial gains by Ottoman empire in the Ukraine; Kara Mustapha appointed Grand Vizier
1593–1606	Frontier wars between Austrians and Turks		
1606–39	Frontier wars between Ottoman and Persian empires	1683	Second unsuccessful Turkish siege of Vienna; execution of Kara Mustapha
1609	Moriscos expelled from Spain	1687	Turks defeated at second battle of Mohacs and driven from Hungary and Serbia
1614–17	Venetian war against the uskoks in the Adriatic		
1618–48	Thirty Years War in Germany	1690	Turks recapture Niš and Belgrade
1622	Janissary mutiny deposes and executes Sultan Osman II	1697	Turks defeated at battle of Zenta
		1699	Treaty of Karlowitz

BIBLIOGRAPHICAL NOTES

Two books dominate the field by reason of the richness of their scholarship and their boldness of interpretation: F. Braudel's masterpiece, *La Méditerranée et le monde méditerranéan à l'époque de Philippe II* (Paris 1949) and W. H. McNeill, *Europe's Steppe Frontier, 1500–1800* (Chicago 1964). A recent short article by Braudel carries some of his ideas a stage further; 'Conjonctures en Méditerrannée au XVIe siècle', in *Mélanges Pierre Renouvin: études d'histoire des relations internationales* (Paris 1966).

On the history of the Ottoman empire there is a choice between three voluminous, old-fashioned but extremely informative works in German: J. F. von Hammer-Purgstall, *Geschichte des osmanischen Reiches* (10 vols, Budapest 1827–35); J. W. Zinkeisen, *Geschichte des osmanischen Reiches in Europa* (7 vols, Hamburg-Gotha 1840–63); and N. Jorga, *Geschichte des osmanischen Reiches* (5 vols, Gotha 1908–13). D. Vaughn, *Europe and the Turk: a pattern of alliances, 1350–1800* (Liverpool 1954) is excellent on the diplomatic accompaniment to Ottoman relations with Europe.

The following general histories of eastern Europe and the Balkan states are uneven in quality, but all are useful at many points: F. Dvornik, *The Slavs in European History and Civilization* (New Brunswick 1962); N. Jorga, *Histoire des états balkaniques jusqu'à 1924* (Paris 1925); R. Ristelhueber, *Histoire des peuples balkaniques* (Paris 1950); L. S. Stavrianos, *The Balkans since 1453* (New York 1958); G. Stadtmüller, *Geschichte Südosteuropas* (Munich 1950); H. Hantsch, *Geschichte Österreichs* (2 vols, Graz 1947); C. A. Macartney, *Hungary: a short history* (Edinburgh 1962); M. Macdermott, *A History of Bulgaria, 1393–1885* (London 1962); A. Otetea et al., eds., *Istoria Rominiei* (Bucharest n.d., *magnificently illustrated*); and N. Jorga, *A History of Roumania* (London 1925). J. Tadic, ed., *Ten Years of Yugoslav Historiography, 1945–1955* (Belgrade 1955) summarizes many relevant monographs and articles.

More specific references follow under the appropriate chapter headings. These are highly selective and compressed; for the most part they record studies which proved particularly helpful or illuminating during the writing of this book. Works in English are given a greater prominence than they really deserve. I am unfortunately linguistically disqualified from consulting books in Turkish, Magyar or the Slav languages.

The standard book on the nomad societies of the steppe is R. Grousset, *L'Empire* *des Steppes* (Paris 1939); this is usefully supplemented by B. Spuler, *Les Mongols dans l'histoire* (Paris 1961) and E. D. Phillips, *The Royal Hordes: Nomad Peoples of the Steppe* (London 1965). P. Witteck, *The Rise of the Ottoman Empire* (London 1938) is lucid and scholarly, an outstanding work; for further detail see H. A. Gibbons, *The Foundation of the Ottoman Empire, 1300–1403* (Oxford 1916); H. H. Schaeder, 'Der Osmanische Staat von seiner Entstehung bis zum Ausgang des siebzehnten Jahrhunderts' in *Propyläen Weltgeschichte*, vol. 5 (Berlin 1930); W. L. Langer and R. P. Blake, 'The Rise of the Ottoman Turks and its Historical Background' in *The American Historical Review* (1932); M. F. Koprülü, *Les origines de l'empire ottoman* (Paris 1935); and F. Taescher, 'The Ottoman Turks to 1453' in *The Cambridge Medieval History*, revised vol. 4 (Cambridge 1965). W. Miller, 'The Medieval Serbian Empire' in *The Quarterly Review* (1916) is good on the Serbian state created by Stephan Dušan. A. S. Atiya, *The Crusade of Nicopolis* (London 1934) draws extensively on source-material in Turkish and Arabic. Sir S. Runciman, *The Fall of Constantinople, 1453* (Cambridge 1965) is a learned and colourful account; D. Stacton, *The World on the Last Day* (London 1965) is also instructive on the same theme. For the continuance of Byzantine traditions after 1453 see N. Jorga, *Byzance après Byzance* (Bucharest 1935). F. Babinger, *Mehmed der Eroberer und seine Zeit* (Munich 1953) is a fine biography of one of the greatest Ottoman sultans. A French translation is available (Paris 1954). On the importance of Caffa and the commerce of the Pontic region see G. I. Bratianu, 'Etudes sur l'approvisionnement de Constantinople et le monopole du blé à l'époque Byzantine et Ottomane' in *Etudes byzantines d'histoire économique et sociale* (Paris 1938); M. Malowist, *Kaffa, kolonia genuenska na Krymic, 1453–1475* (with résumé in French, Warsaw 1947); and M. Lombard, 'Caffa et la fin de la route mongole' in *Annales* (1949). A. Gegaj, *L'Albanie et l'invasion turque au XVe siècle* (Paris 1937), though restricted in scope, is the best single study of early Ottoman imperialism in the Balkans.

H. A. R. Gibb and H. Bowen, *Islamic Society and the West* (2 vols, Oxford 1950, 1957) is a fundamental work of reference and interpretation. R. Levy, *The Social Structure of Islam* (Cambridge 1957) is illuminating at many points, especially on the role of slavery in the Moslem world. N. Ernst, 'Die ersten Einfälle der Krim Tartaren auf Süd-Russland' in *Zeitschrift für Osteuropäische Geschichte* (1913) gives details on Tartar slave-raiding in Pontic Europe. A. H. Lybyer, *The Government of the Ottoman Empire in the Time of Suleiman the Magnificent* (Harvard 1913), the very thorough standard work on institutions, is weak on the relationship between these and social movements; the same author, 'Constantinople as Capital of the Ottoman

Empire' in *Annual Report of the American Historical Association* (1916) does something to remedy this deficiency. For special aspects of the sultanate see W.L. Wright, ed., *Ottoman Statecraft* (Princeton 1935), and A.D. Alderson, *The Structure of the Ottoman Dynasty* (Oxford 1956). O.L. Barkan, 'Essai sur les données statistiques des registres de recensement dans l'empire Ottoman aux XVᵉ et XVIᵉ siècles' in *Journal of the Economic and Social History of the Orient* (1958) is invaluable on the difficult problem of population, and R. Busch-Zantner, *Agrarverfassung, Gesellschaft und Siedlung in Südosteuropa* (Leipzig 1938) is essential for an understanding of the rural economy of the European provinces. The place of gilds in Ottoman social and economic life is explored by F. Taeschner, 'Beiträge zur Geschichte der Achis in Anatolien' in *Islamica* (1929), and B. Lewis, 'The Islamic Guilds' in *The Economic History Review* (1937). The best study of the janissaries is T. Menzel, 'Das Korps der Janitscharen' in *Beiträge zur Kenntnis des Orients* (Berlin 1902-3); another monograph on military history with wide implications beyond its restricted field is D. Ayalon, *Gunpowder and Firearms in the Mamluk Kingdom* (London 1956). On problems of religion see D. B. Macdonald. *The Development of Muslim Theology, Jurisprudence and Constitutional Theory* (London 1903); F. W. Hasluck, *Christianity and Islam under the Sultans* (2 vols, Oxford 1929); Sir T. Arnold, ed., *The Legacy of Islam* (Oxford 1931); and J.K. Birge, *The Bektashi Order of Dervishes* (London 1937). The quotations from Ziya Gökalp may be found in his *Turkish Nationalism and Western Civilization* (ed. and transl. N. Berkes, London 1959).

THE WARS AGAINST THE WEST There are two biographies of Suleiman the Magnificent: F. Babinger, *Suleyman der Grosse* (2 vols, Stuttgart 1922) and R.B. Merriman, *Suleiman the Magnificent* (Harvard 1944). K. Brandi, *The Emperor Charles V* (transl. C. V. Wedgwood, London 1939), and P. Rassow, *Die politische Welt Karls V* (Berlin 1947), are the best studies of his principal European opponent. V.J. Parry, 'The Ottoman Empire, 1520-1566' in *The New Cambridge Modern History*, vol. 2 (Cambridge 1958) is a vivid, concise and authoritative survey. On the situation in Hungary there are four books in the best tradition of nineteenth-century German scholarship: W. Fraknoi, *Ungarn vor der Schlacht bei Mohacz, 1524-1526* (Budapest 1886); the same author, *Matthias Corvinus, König von Ungarn, 1458-1490* (Freiburg-im-Breisgau 1891); F. Salamon, *Ungarn im Zeitalter der Türkenherrschaft* (Leipzig 1887); and L. Kupelweiser, *Die Kämpfe Ungarns mit den Osmanen bis zur Schlacht bei Mohacs* (Vienna 1899). For military operations see B. Chudoba, *Spain and the Empire, 1519-1643* (New York 1953); H. Inalchik, 'Ottoman methods of conquest' in *Studia Islamica* (1954); and G. E. Rothenberg, *The Austrian Military Border in Croatia, 1522-1747* (Urbana, Illinois 1960). Braudel *op. cit.* overshadows all other writing on the Mediterranean naval wars, but the following are also worth consulting: L. von Ranke, 'Die Osmanen und die Spanische Monarchie' in *Sämtliche Werke*, vol. xxxv/vi (Leipzig 1877); Sir W. Stirling-Maxwell, *Don John of Austria* (2 vols, London 1883); J. de la Gravière, *Doria et Barbérousse* (Paris 1886); J. Ursu, *La politique orientale de François I* (Paris 1908); L. Serrano, *La Liga de Lepanto* (2 vols, Madrid 1918, 1920); P. Kahle, ed., *Das Türkische Segelhandbuch für das Mittelländische Meer vom Jahre 1521* (Berlin-Leipzig 1926); Ch.-A. Julien, *Histoire de l'Afrique du Nord* (Paris 1931); R. C. Anderson, *Naval Wars in the Levant* (Liverpool 1952); and Sir G. Fisher, *Barbary Legend: War, Trade and Piracy in North Africa, 1415–1830* (Oxford 1957). There is a reliable summary treatment by an historian familiar with the Spanish sources in J. Lynch, *Spain under the Habsburgs* (vol. I): *Empire and Absolutism, 1516–1598* (Oxford 1963).

For up-to-date discussions of the Middle Eastern spice trade after the Turkish conquest of Syria and Egypt see P. Sardella, *Nouvelles et spéculations à Venise au début du XVIe siècle* (Paris 1948) and V. M. Godhino, 'Le repli vénitien et égyptien et la route du Cap' in *Eventail de l'Histoire Vivante: Hommage à Lucien Febvre*, vol. 2 (Paris 1953). On the European provinces and client states of the Ottoman empire the following are useful: L. Villari, *The Republic of Ragusa* (London 1904); J. Tadic, 'La part de Raguse au commerce méditerranéen au XVIe siècle' in *Atti del Xe Congresso Internazionale di Scienze Storiche* (Rome 1955); B. Krekic, *Dubrovnik (Raguse) et le Levant au moyen âge* (Paris-The Hague 1961); L. Hadrovics, *Le peuple serbe et son église sous la domination turque* (Paris 1947); T. H. Papadopoulos, *Studies and documents relating to the history of the Greek church and people under Turkish dominion* (Brussels 1952); and L. Makkai, *Histoire de Transylvanie* (Paris 1946). For anyone able to read Serbo-Croat H. Kreševljakovič, *Banje u Bosni i Hercegovini* (Sarajevo 1952), contains interesting information on urbanization in the Balkans under Ottoman rule. Two essays by R. R. Betts, 'The Reformation in difficulties: Poland, Bohemia and Hungary' and 'Constitutional Development and Political Thought in Eastern Europe' in *The New Cambridge Modern History*, vol. 2 (Cambridge 1958) are excellent on the effects of the battle of Mohacs on religious life in Hungary and on the administrative reforms of Ferdinand I in the Habsburg portion of the kingdom. Essential perspectives on Spain are provided by F. Braudel, 'Les Espagnols et l'Afrique du Nord de 1492 à 1577' in *Revue Africaine* (1928); J. M. Doussinague, *La política exterior de España en el siglo XVI* (Madrid 1949); J. Sanchez Montes, *Franceses, Protestantes, Turcos. Los españoles ane la política internacional de Carlos V* (Madrid 1951); J. Vicens Vives, 'La Corona de Aragón y el ámbito del Mediterraneo Occidental durante la época de Carlos V' in *Karl V, der Kaiser und seine Zeit* (Cologne 1960); and J. H. Elliot, *Imperial Spain*,

1469–1716 (London 1964). H. G. Koenigsberger, *The Government of Sicily under Philip II of Spain* (London-New York 1951) is invaluable on a strategically situated Spanish colony. The best discussions of the morisco problem are P. Boronat, *Los moriscos españoles y su expulsión* (2 vols, Valencia 1901); H. C. Lea, *The Moriscos of Spain* (Philadelphia 1901); J. Reglá, 'La cuestión morisca y la coyuntura internacional en tiempos de Felipe II' in *Estudios de Historia Moderna* (1953); and J. Caro Baroja, *Los moriscos del reino de Granada* (Madrid 1957). From a vast literature on Venice the following are particularly relevant: R. Fulin, 'I Portoghesi in India e i Veneziani in Egitto' in *Archivio Veneto* (1881); H. Kretschmayr, *Geschichte von Venedig*, vol. 2 (Gotha 1920); P. Sardella, 'L'épanouissement industriel de Venise au XVIe siècle' in *Annales* (1947); F. Sassi, 'La politica navale veneziana dopo Lepanto' in *Archivio Veneto* (1946–7); G. Luzzatto, 'La decadenza di Venezia dopo le scoperte geografiche nella tradizione e nella realtà' in *Archivio Veneto* (1954); F. Thiriet, 'Les lettres commerciales des Bembo et le commerce vénitien dans l'empire ottoman à la fin du XVe siècle' in *Studi in onore di Armando Sapori* (Milan 1957); A. Tenenti, *Venezia e i corsari* (Bari 1961); and the same author, *Cristoforo da Canal: la marine vénitienne avant Lépante* (Paris 1962). H. G. Rawlinson, 'The Embassy of William Harborne to Constantinople, 1583–8' in *Transactions of the Royal Historical Society* (1922), records the self-confidence and success of the English challenge to Venetian commerce in the eastern Mediterranean. Genoa has been less well served by historians: the monumental study by J. Heers, *Gênes au XVe siècle* (Paris 1961) may be supplemented by H. Sieveking, *Genueser Finanzwesen mit besonderer Berücksichtigung der Casa di San Giorgio* (Fribourg 1898); R. Lopez, 'Il predominio economico dei Genovesi nella monarchia spagnuola' in *Giornale storico e letterario della Liguria* (1936); R. Carande, *Carlos V y sus banqueros*, vol. 2 (Madrid 1949); R. Romano, 'Banchieri genovesi alla corte di Filippo II' in *Rivista Storica Italiana* (1949); and P. Argenti, *The Occupation of Chios by the Genoese* (3 vols, Cambridge 1958). The wide variety of European reactions to Turkish expansion is well illustrated in C. D. Rouillard, *The Turk in French History, Thought and Literature, 1520–1660* (Paris 1938); F. L. Baumer, 'England, the Turk and the Common Corps of Christendom' in *The American Historical Review* (1945); H. Pfefferman, *Die Zusammenarbeit der Renaissancepäpste mit den Türken* (Winterthur 1946); and S. Fischer-Galati, *Ottoman Imperialism and German Protestantism* (Harvard 1959). For discussion of the relationship between Ottoman aggression and the crystallization of the idea of Europe see *Actes du Colloque International sur la Notion d'Europe* (Paris 1963) and J. B. Duroselle, *L'idée d'Europe dans l'histoire* (Paris 1965). Interesting accounts of the sixteenth-century Ottoman empire by two of the handful of European visitors who were capable of reporting dispassionately on what they saw are *The Turkish Letters of Ogier Ghislain de Busbecq* (transl. E. S.

Forster, Oxford 1927) and Philippe du Fresne-Canaye, *Le Voyage du Levant* (ed. M.H.Hauser, Paris 1897). There are picaresque descriptions of Mediterranean warfare against the Turks in the memoirs of two Spanish adventurers: C. de Villalón, *Viaje de Turquía* (2 vols, Madrid-Barcelona 1919) and *Vida del capitan Alonso de Contreras* (ed. Sarrano y Sanz, Madrid 1900); the text of the latter is also available in French (1911). On the extraordinary career of Joseph Nasi and for much detail on the life of Jewish communities in Constantinople and other cities see C.Roth, *The House of Nasi: The Duke of Naxos* (Philadelphia 1949) and M. Franco, *Essai sur l'histoire des Israelites de l'empire Ottoman depuis les origines jusqu'à nos jours* (Paris 1897).

There is no comprehensive book either on the exhaustion of Ottoman imperialism in Europe or on the Kuprülü revival, but the following essays are of uniformly high quality: S.J.Shaw, 'The Ottoman View of the Balkans' in *The Balkans in Transition* (ed. C. and B.Jelavich, Berkeley, California 1963); T.Stoianovich, 'Land tenure and related sectors of the Balkan economy' in *The Journal of Economic History* (1953); the same author, 'The Conquering Balkan Orthodox Merchant' in *The Journal of Economic History* (1960); and H.Inalchik, 'Land Problems in Turkish History' in *The Muslim World* (1955). For references to the role of Albanians see M.E.Durham, *Some Tribal Origins, Laws and Customs of the Balkans* (London 1928) and G.Stadtmüller, 'Die albanische Volkstumsgeschichte als Forschungsproblem' in *Leipziger Vierteljahrschrift für Südosteuropa* (1941–2). W.E.D.Allen, *The Ukraine: a History* (Cambridge 1940) is first-class on developments in this area. A.F.Pribram, *Franz Paul von Lisola und die Politik seiner Zeit* (Vienna 1894) is good on Austrian policy. Three studies transcend the naive and disputatious patriotism which generally disfigures the historiography of Hungary: H.Marczali, *Ungarische Verfassungsgeschichte* (Tübingen 1910); C.d'Eszlary, 'L'administration et la vie dans la Hongrie occupée par les Turcs au cours des XVIe et XVIIe siècles' in *Ibla, Revue d'instituts des belles-lettres arabes* (1956); and A.N.J.Hollander, 'The Great Hungarian Plain: a European Frontier Area' in *Comparative Studies in Society and History* (1960–1). A.Lefaivre, *Les Magyars pendant la domination ottomane en Hongrie, 1526–1722* (Paris 1902), is valuable for detail but for nothing else. For the last great Ottoman offensive in Europe see R.F.Kreutel, *Kara Mustafa vor Wien* (Graz 1955), and J.Stoye, *The Siege of Vienna* (London 1964). On technology and the changing balance of military power C.M.Cipolla, *Guns and Sails in the early phase of European Exploration* (London 1965), shows what an unconventional but thoroughly professional economic historian can achieve when he applies his talents to a field normally tilled only by enthusiastic amateurs.

LIST OF ILLUSTRATIONS

24 Sweepers in the Hippodrome, Constanti-
nople. *Surnama* of Murad III (1574–95).
Topkapi Saray Library, Istanbul. *Photo: Wim
Swaan.*

25 *Kazi-Asker* (Judge-Advocate). Wood-
engraving by Melchior Lorch from *Costumes
. . .*, 1570–83, fol. 191. British Museum.
Photo: Freeman.

26 Khurrem, consort of Suleiman the Magnificent. Wood-engraving by Melchior Lorch
from *Costumes . . .*, 1570–83, fol. 172. British
Museum. *Photo: Freeman.*

27 Black eunuch, slave of the Virgins, super-
intendent of the Palace of Women. Turkish
miniature, from *A breife relation of the Turckes*,
by Peter Mundy, 1618. British Museum.
Photo: Fleming.

28 Beglerbeg. From *A breife relation of the
Turckes*, 1618. *The Trustees of the British
Museum.*

29 Christian child taken to be trained as
janissary. From *A breife relation of the
Turckes*, 1618. *The Trustees of the British
Museum.*

30 Plan of Constantinople by Buondelmonte,
1453. *The Trustees of the British Museum.*

31 View of Constantinople. From Braun and
Hohenberg, *Civitates Orbis Terrarum*, 1572.
British Museum. *Photo: Freeman.*

32 Ottoman camp in Georgia. Miniature from
Nusretname. Turkish, 1582. British Museum.
Photo: Fleming.

33 *Azapi* (common foot soldier). Wood-
engraving by Melchior Lorch from *Costumes
. . .*, 1570–83, fol. 183. British Museum.
Photo: Freeman.

34 Sipahi. Wood-engraving by Melchior Lorch
from *Costumes . . .*, 1570–83, fol. 193. British
Museum. *Photo: Freeman.*

35 Moorish soldier. Wood-engraving by Melchior Lorch from *Costumes . . .*, 1570–83,
fol. 182. British Museum. *Photo: Freeman.*

36 Slave market in Constantinople. From *Het
Ellendigh Leven der Turcken*, 1663. British
Museum. *Photo: Freeman.*

37 Procession in Constantinople, 1648. From
Coecke van Elst, *Les Moeurs et fachons de faire*

de Turcs, 1533. British Museum. *Photo:
Freeman.*

38 Mevlevi dervishes, Turkish miniature, from
a mid-seventeenth century MS, probably
executed for a Venetian ambassador. Private
collection.

39 The Battle of Mohacs, 1526. After the copy
of 1545 of the miniature of Dzelábiade
Mustapha, Tabarat-ul-memálik. National
Museum, Budapest.

40 The Victory of Mohacs. From the *Hünerame*
(Book of Exploits) compiled by Lokman
with miniatures by Osman. Sixteenth century. Topkapi Sarayi Museum, Istanbul.

41 Janissary. From N. de Nicolay. *Navigations et
Peregrinations*, 1568. British Museum. *Photo:
Freeman.*

42 Camp life, Turkish miniature from a mid-
seventeenth century MS, probably executed
for a Venetian ambassador. Private collection.

43 Turkish prostitute. From N. de Nicolay,
Navigations et Peregrinations, 1568. British
Museum. *Photo: Freeman.*

44 Drowning janissaries. Detail from miniature
in *Nusretname*, showing Mustapha Pasha
crossing the river Kur. Turkish, 1582. British
Museum. *Photo: Fleming.*

45 Ismail Safavi. Wood-engraving by Melchior
Lorch, 1557. British Museum, Department of
Prints and Drawings. *Photo: Freeman.*

46 Ismail Safavi in battle against the king of
Shirvan, Persian, 1541. British Museum.
Photo: Freeman.

47 Battle between Turks (Selim I) and Persians
in Calimania, 1514. From *Von der Schlacht
geschehem dem Turcken*, 1594. British Museum.
Photo: Freeman.

48 Turks on stilts in the snow, Belgrade. From
Marvels of Art and Nature, Turkish, c. 1550–75.
British Museum. *Photo: Fleming.*

49 Matthias Corvinus. From T. Mueller,
Musaei Joviana Imagines, 1577. British
Museum. *Photo: Freeman.*

50 Ladislas V. From Terzio, *Imagines Austriacae
Gentis*, Innsbruck 1558. National Museum,
Budapest.

79 View of Venice. From Hartmann Schedel, *Liber chronicarum*, Nuremburg 1493. British Museum. *Photo: Freeman.*

80 View of Genoa. From Braun and Hohenberg, *Civitates Orbis Terrarum*, Vol. 1, no. 45, 1572. British Museum. *Photo: Freeman.*

81 Gian-Andrea Doria. From an engraving. Copyright Ashmolean Museum, Department of Western Art, Oxford.

82 Title page of Martin Luther's *Eine Heer predigt widder den Turken*, Wittenberg, 1529. British Museum. *Photo: Freeman.*

83 Chained captive Christians. From B. Georgevich, *De afflictione tam captivorum*, 1544. British Museum. *Photo: Freeman.*

84 Punishment of fugitives. From B. Georgevich, *De afflictione tam captivorum*, 1544. British Museum. *Photo: Freeman.*

85 Paolo Giovio. Portrait by an anonymous artist, sixteenth century. Uffizi Gallery, Florence. *Photo: Mansell Collection.*

86 Busbecq. Engraving by Melchior Lorch. British Museum, Department of Prints and Drawings. *Photo: Freeman.*

87 Title page of Thomas Fuller's *The Historie of the Holy Warre*, 1639. British Museum. *Photo: Freeman.*

88 Genealogy of the Ottoman rulers. From F. Sansovino, *Sommario et Alboro delli principi Othomani*, 1567. British Museum. *Photo: Freeman.*

89 Gracia Nasi. Medal by Pastorino, with a Hebrew inscription. Bibliothèque Nationale, Paris.

90 Jewish doctor. From N. de Nicolay, *Navigations et Peregrinations*, 1568. British Museum. *Photo: Freeman.*

91 Sultan Selim II shooting an arrow, with a page, by Reis Maydar, called Nigari (1494–1572). Portrait Gallery, Topkapi Museum, Istanbul.

92 Siege of Vienna, 1683 (detail). Painting by Franz Geffel, late seventeenth century. Museum der Stadt Wien. *Photo: Meyer, Vienna.*

93 Ottoman troops occupying Tiflis (August 1578). Miniature from *Nusretname*, Turkish, 1582. British Museum. *Photo: Fleming.*

94 Amulet, 'the hand of Fatima', found at Sarajevo. Brass with arabic lettering.

95 Mohammed III. Anonymous painting. *Photo: Ullstein Bilderdienst.*

96 The battle of the Dardanelles (detail), by Peitro Liberi. Palazzo Ducale, Venice. *Photo: Mansell Collection.*

97 Plan of the battle of St Gothard, 1664. Heeresgeschichtliches Museum, Vienna.

98 John III Sobieski, King of Poland (1629–96). From an engraving. *Photo: Mansell Collection.*

99 Field-Marshal Raimondo Montecuccoli. Painting reproduced by courtesy of Ray Thompson, Esq.

100 Imre Tökölli, from Tökölli, *Warhaffte eigentliche Original-Bildnis*, 1683. British Museum. *Photo: Freeman.*

101 Kara Mustapha. Engraving. British Museum, Department of Prints and Drawings. *Photo Freeman.*

102 The execution of Kara Mustapha, 1683. British Museum, Department of Prints and Drawings. *Photo: Freeman.*

103 The Treaty of Karlowitz, 2 March 1699. Bildarchiv d. Öst. Nationalbibliothek, Vienna.

104 Prince Eugene of Savoy. Portrait by Jacques von Schuppen. Rijksmuseum, Amsterdam.

105 Turkish cannon, brass; fifteenth century. Tower of London. *Photo: Ministry of Public Building and Works* (Crown Copyright reserved). Reproduced by permission of the Master of the Armouries.

106 Armenian merchant, from N. de Nicolay, *Navigations et Peregrinations*, 1568. British Museum. *Photo: Freeman.*

107 Jewish merchant, from N. de Nicolay, *Navigations et Peregrinations*, 1568. British Museum. *Photo: Freeman.*

108 Title page of R. Knolles, *The Generall Historie of the Turkes*, 1603. British Museum. *Photo: Freeman.*

109 Coffee house outside the walls of Vienna. From a seventeenth-century engraving by I. A. Delsenbach. *Photo: Bildarchiv d. Öst. Nationalbibliothek, Vienna.*

The map on pages 8–9 was drawn by S. Schotten.

INDEX

Page numbers in italics refer to illustrations

214

Uskoks 103, 138
Uskub (*see* Skopje)
Usodimare 143

Valencia 127–9
Vasco da Gama 107
Vasvar, truce of 178
Vega, Juan de 126
Venice, Venetians 16, 49, 78, 92,
  93, 94, 97, 98, 99, 101, 104, 108,
  110, 111, 131–9, 160, 174, 176,
  178–9, 183–4, *132–3, 135*
Verböczy, Istvan 81
Vidin 183
Vienna 7, 71, 85, 86, 102, 103, 110,
  119–23, 160, 180–2, 183, 191, 194,
  85, 86, 160, 195

Visegrad 87
Vlachs 114, 115

Wallachia 80, 114, 132, 173–4, 176,
  183
Walloons 120
Walsingham 149–50
Westphalia, Treaty of 173
Wittenberg 68

Zadé, Mustapha 183–4
Zamanja, Marin 112
Zapolyai, John 81, 85, 86, 87, 181,
  85
Zeno, Pietro 133
Zenta, Battle of 160, 184
Zuravno, Treaty of 179